GLOBALIZATION AND REGIONALIZATION

Challenges for Public Policy

GLOBALIZATION AND REGIONALIZATION

Challenges for Public Policy

edited by

David B. Audretsch
and
Charles F. Bonser

Indiana University

SPRINGER SCIENCE+BUSINESS MEDIA, LLC

Library of Congress Cataloging-in-Publication Data

Globalization and regionalization: challenges for public policy / edited by David B. Audretsch and Charles F. Bonser.

p. cm.

Includes bibliographical references.

ISBN 978-1-4613-5278-5 ISBN 978-1-4615-0867-0 (eBook)

DOI 10.1007/978-1-4615-0867-0

1. Globalization. 2. Regionalization (International organization). I. Audretsch, David B. II. Bonser, Charles F.

JZ1318 .G585 2001 2001050397

327.1—dc21

Originally published by Kluwer Academic Publishers in 2002

Softcover reprint of the hardcover 1st edition 2002

Printed on acid-free paper.

Table of Contents

Chapter 1	*Globalization and Regionalization: Introduction* David B. Audretsch and Charles F. Bonser	1
Chapter 2	*Globalization, Democracy, and New Approaches to Governance in the United States* Alfred C. Aman, Jr.	9
Chapter 3	*Reaching Out to Regional Government in England?* Kenneth Spencer	23
Chapter 4	*Globalization and Changes in Industrial Concentration: State and Regional Exports from America's Heartland, 1988–1997* Lawrence S. Davidson	49
Chapter 5	*Globalization and the Local University* John W. Ryan	71
Chapter 6	*Globalization and the Strategic Management of Regions* David B. Audretsch and A. Roy Thurik	77
Chapter 7	*Living Apart Together in Europe* Jean-Pierre van Aubel and Frans K.M. van Nispen	97
Chapter 8	*The Changing Nature of Regulation: Some Observations from a Southern European Perspective* Montserrat Cuchillo	105
Chapter 9	*Global Trade Sovereignty and Subnational Autonomy* David Eaton	115

Chapter 1:

GLOBALIZATION AND REGIONALIZATION: INTRODUCTION

David B. Audretsch and Charles F. Bonser
Institute for Development Strategies, Indiana University

THE TRANS-ATLANTIC PUBLIC POLICY AGENDA

The beginning of the 21st century finds the Atlantic Alliance partners in evolution toward a new relationship in the key policy arenas of economic and social development, international security, international trade and competition, and the need to deal effectively with environmental and public health problems associated with an expanding global marketplace. The problems associated with these issues have strained relations between Europe and North America. This has been exacerbated by internal preoccupations on both continents that have reduced communication opportunities, and led to misunderstandings on both sides of the Atlantic. It is clear to both the leadership of the European Union and the United States that this potential estrangement is not in the interests of either continent.

In response to this situation, the Clinton Administration and the European Union initiated in December 1995 a series of efforts under the framework of a *New Transatlantic Agenda*. The purpose of these efforts was to strengthen the communication and ties between the EU and the United States in a variety of functional areas. The effort has been largely successful in improving the situation. While agreements may not always be forthcoming, at least communications are more open.

In an effort to contribute to this dialog, in the summer of 1997, the Indiana University School of Public and Environmental Affairs (SPEA), as part of its 25th Anniversary Celebration, co-sponsored an international conference on transatlantic public policy issues with the École Nationale d'Administration (ENA) in Paris, France. The themes of the conference were, "Development and Security Issues for the EU and the US in the 21st century" and "The Next Generation of World Trade Issues." In addition to our faculty and staffs, we included several content experts and public policy leaders in the program from both Europe and the United States.

The conference was quite successful, and many of the participants argued strongly that we should continue this type of joint activity on transatlantic policy issues. As a result, SPEA and ENA developed a plan that would continue these programs, but that would bring several other public policy/administration academic programs in Europe and the US into the process.

A second colloquium on transatlantic issues was held at Indiana University in Bloomington, Indiana, September 30-October 2, 1998. This time the topic was: "Globalization and the Environment." Participating in that colloquium, in addition to ENA and SPEA, were: the German government's Bundesacademie (Bonn, Germany), the University Pompeu Fabra (Barcelona), the National School of Administrative Sciences (Speyer, Germany), the Netherlands School of Government, the Erasmus University School of Social Sciences (Netherlands), the Instituto Nacional de Administracao (Lisbon, Portugal), and the Fondazione Eni E Mattei (Milan, Italy). Once again, the participants included both faculty and outside experts from the various countries involved.

The style of this colloquium—and the group's preference for future meetings—was a roundtable format that limited attendance, and allowed plenty of time for informal exchanges and the building of personal as well as institutional networks. The decision was also made to expand the number of institutions participating in the consortium to include a roughly equal number of American and European organizations. Subsequently, about 25 institutions were invited to attend the next colloquium of the group, which was held at the European Institute for Public Administration in Maastricht, The Netherlands, May 22–26, 2000. Twenty-one institutions from eight nations were represented at the Maastricht meeting. (The institutions participating in the Consortium at present are listed below.)

The institutional representatives met in Maastricht to consider the details of organizing the consortium, as well as other matters of consortium activities. A draft of a consortium agreement was discussed and revised for presentation to the entire group at the conclusion of the colloquium. The agreement to establish the *Transatlantic Consortium for Public Policy Analysis and Education* was unanimously adopted May 25, 2000. Charles F. Bonser was chosen the first Chair of the Consortium. The Institute for Development Strategies at Indiana

University was designated the Secretariat of the organization. An Executive Committee to oversee the affairs of the Consortium between membership meetings was appointed. The members of the Committee are: Montserrat Cuchillo, Pompeu Fabra University, Barcelona, Spain; Kenneth Spencer, University of Birmingham, UK; Frank Thompson, Albany Campus, State University of New York; Leigh Boske, University of Texas; and Juergen von Hagen, University of Bonn, Germany.

The Consortium agreed early in its deliberations that the intellectual content of its colloquia, focused on public policy issues of concern to the Transatlantic Alliance between the United States and the European Union, should be shared more broadly with scholars and policy makers concerned with transatlantic policy issues. As a result, the decision was made to develop a publication series that would be based on the colloquia of the organization. An agreement was subsequently reached with Kluwer Academic Publishers to publish the papers and summary discussions of the first two colloquia. This publication, edited by Charles F. Bonser, was released in March of 2000, under the title: *Security, Trade, and Environmental Policy: A US/European Union Agenda*.

This volume is therefore the second in the colloquia series. The theme of the Maastricht colloquium was, "Globalization and Regionalization: A Paradoxical Challenge for Public Policy." Keynote addresses were given by Mikel Landabasco, of the European Commission, and Cynthia P. Schneider, US Ambassador to the Netherlands. Papers were presented, and discussions held, on the topics: Globalization and the Local University; The Changing Nature of Regulation; Globalization, Competitiveness and the Shift to the Entrepreneurial Economy; Federalism, Globalization, and Europe; The Changing Role of Government; and Governance in Globalized World.

The next colloquium of the Consortium is scheduled to be held September 20-22, 2001, at the University of Pittsburgh. The theme selected for the Colloquium is: "Ethics, Accountability, and Social Responsibility—A Transatlantic Perspective."

As of December 2000, the institutions working together in the Consortium are:

In the United States:

Indiana University (The School of Public and Environmental Affairs, The Kelley School of Business, and the School of Law)
Syracuse University (The Maxwell School of Citizenship and Public Affairs)
University of Texas (The Lyndon B. Johnson School of Public Affairs)
American University (School of Public Affairs)
State University of New York at Albany (School of Public Administration)
The University of Pittsburgh (School of Public and International Affairs)

Carnegie Mellon University (Heinz School of Public and Urban Affairs)
The University of Southern California (School of Policy, Planning, and Development
Florida International University (School of Public Affairs)
University of Maryland (School of Public Affairs)
University of Georgia (Department of Political Science and the Institute of Government)

In Europe
École Nationale d'Administration, Paris, France
International Institute of Public Administration, Paris, France
The University of Paris–Sorbonne (Faculties of Law and Public Administration)
Erasmus University, Rotterdam, The Netherlands
Leiden University, The Netherlands
Netherlands School of Government
Federal Academy of Public Administration, Bonn, Germany
National School of Administrative Sciences, Speyer, Germany
University of Bonn, Germany (Center for European Integration)
Instituto Nacional de Administracio, Lisbon, Portugal
University Pompeu Fabra, Barcelona, Spain
Jonkoping University, Sweden
Institute for Technology Assessment and Systems Analysis, Karlsruhe, Germany
London School of Economics (Department of Political Science)
University of Birmingham, United Kingdom (School of Public Affairs)
Danish School of Public Administration, Denmark

A preliminary consortium web site has been developed and is in the process of being refined. The address for the web site is <http://www.spea.indiana.edu/tac/>. This site now contains basic information about the consortium, as well as providing web links to the home pages of several of the consortium members.

GLOBALIZATION AND REGIONALIZATION

In recent years there has been a good deal of attention paid to the increasing globalization of the world economy and its socio/political systems. In its most general use, it can be said that globalization refers to all the phenomena at work in today's society that reduce the ability of a nation to control its own actions and institutions. In his book, *The Lexus and the Olive Tree*, Thomas Friedman describes globalization as "the constant revolutionalizing of production, and the endless disturbance of all social conditions."

Trade liberalization—resulting from the eight General Agreement on Tariffs and Trade (GATT) negotiation rounds that took place between 1948 and 1995—

has led to substantial reductions in tariffs and trade barriers in a trading system that in 1999 included 123 member country signatories to the GATT. Since 1988, trade has increased twice as fast as output, and foreign direct investment has grown three times as fast.

The world volume of trade has increased by nearly 400 percent between 1970 and 1997. Over this same period global production has only doubled. In the most developed countries the increase in trade has been even greater. For example, exports as a share of gross domestic product for 49 developed countries has risen from around 18 percent in 1982 to around 25 percent by 1999. Similarly, real exports have increased in the United States from $86.8 billion in 1960, to $818.0 billion in 1996. At the same time, real imports have risen from $108.1 billion to 883.0 billion.

The increase in world trade is also not attributable to the influence of just a few industries or sectors, but rather systematic across most parts of the economy. The exposure to foreign competition in manufacturing increased by about one-sixth in the OECD countries. The exposure to foreign competition increased in every single OECD country, with the exception of Japan. In addition, it increased in most of the manufacturing industries.

A different manifestation of globalization involves foreign direct investment, which has increased by 700 percent between 1970 and 1997 for the entire world. The increase in global FDI has also not been solely the result of a greater participation by countries previously excluded from the world economy. FDI as a percentage of GDP increased in the 1970s, 1980s and 1990s for the major economies of the US and the engine of the European economy, Germany. In the US, annual FDI represented slightly more than 1 percent of GDP during the 1970s. In the 1980s, this had risen to around 1.2 percent. By the 1990s, annual FDI was more than 1.5 percent of GDP. For the United States, outward foreign direct investment increased from $1,637.1 billion in 1987 to $2,931.9 billion in 1995. Inward foreign direct investment into the United States increased from $1,385.9 billion to $3,745.9 billion over this same time period.

Trans-national capital flows have also increased in the past two decades. The value of bonds and equities involved in cross-border transactions has exploded over the past two decades for the six of the largest economies. In addition, the amount of foreign exchange traded has also increased. The cross-border transactions in bonds and equities as a percentage of GDP rose in the US from 9.0 percent in 1980 to 135.5 percent by 1995. In Italy, the increase was from 1.1 percent to 250.9 percent, and in Germany from 7.5 percent to 168.3 percent.

While the magnitudes have obviously changed, it is worth recognizing that globalization is not really something new. It has been going on for a long time. One hundred and fifty years ago, foreign direct investment, as a percentage of Gross Domestic Product (GDP), was very high for many European nations. World

Trade, as a percentage of GDP, was almost as high before World War I as it is now. The movement of labor from one country to another (then heavily east to west) was more important in the 19th century than it is today, when migration is more south to north. For many countries, trade as a percentage of GDP, has not changed much over the past 40 years.

So if globalization is not all that new a phenomenon, what dynamics have changed? What is different that has driven up the above described trade measures in a relatively short period, has attracted so much attention, and how is this affecting the so-called "New Economy," and the demography of production. The answer appears to be that *the interaction between a more open trading system and the new telecommunications and computer technology, has substantially increased productivity and facilitated the fragmentation of the production process.*

The fragmentation of the production process has resulted in a new international organization of production. It has accelerated the globalization of national economies and has allowed firms to take advantage of low wages, wherever they are to be found, and, where important, to locate production facilities close to their customers. Today, the employers seem more mobile than the employees.

This expansion in international trade and production mobility has resulted in at least three sources of gain to the new economy:

1. As the market available to be served by producers expands from a national to an international market, there are gains resulting from declining costs per unit of production.

2. Gains result from decreased monopolistic power of domestic producers and increased competition from foreign producers, as domestic producers are forced to produce the output demanded by consumers at the lowest possible cost, thereby helping keep inflation under control.

3. Consumers gain from the increased variety, quality, and lower prices resulting from the increased competition in a more open world market.

CONTENTS OF THIS VOLUME

In the second chapter of this volume, Alfred C. Aman, Jr. examines whether globalization dictates new approaches to governance. The process by which public policy in England has incorporated regional government is the focus of Kenneth Spencer in Chapter 3. In the third chapter Lawrence S. Davidson provides an analysis of the impact of globalization on manufacturing in the US Midwest. In

Chapter 5, John W. Ryan shows how there is a dual role of universities in the global economy. On the one hand, universities serve as institutions that foster globalization and reduce the isolation of regions. On the other hand, universities themselves are shaped and influenced by globalization. David B. Audretsch and A. Roy Thurik, in Chapter 6, show how globalization has led to the emergence of the strategic management of regions. In Chapter 7, Jean -Pierre van Aubel and Frans van Nispen examines the links between federalization and globalization in the European context. The impact of globalization on regulatory institutions is the focus of Montserrat Cuchillo in Chapter 8. Finally, in Chapter 9, David Eaton examines the relationship between global trade sovereignty and subnational autonomy.

Taken together, these chapters provide a compelling view that public policy must be considered in a new light in the global economy. Not only does policy have to consider global implications, but also the increasing importance of local characteristics and regional strengths.

Chapter 2:

GLOBALIZATION, DEMOCRACY, AND NEW APPROACHES TO GOVERNANCE IN THE UNITED STATES

Alfred C. Aman, Jr.
Indiana University School of Law—Bloomington

Introduction

New approaches to governance in the United States will be closely tied to the ways in which lawmakers conceptualize globalization. This is because global processes—be they economic, social, or cultural—all directly affect the roles states play in various regulatory arenas at home and abroad. The impact of global processes on markets and states contributes to the basic political economy framework within which various regulatory reforms have developed and will develop in the future. The underlying basis of these effects provides the theoretical structure within which approaches to governance evolve, opening the way to new approaches at domestic and international levels of governance. In this essay, I will focus primarily on some of the domestic regulatory changes now occurring in the US and their relationship to globalization. I will concentrate, in particular, on the risk of increasing the democracy deficit that globalization encourages and I will make three proposals to mitigate the negative effects of globalization on governance at the domestic level.[1]

The processes of globalization that now dominate the political economies of most developed and many developing countries have promoted new roles for states and new approaches to issues ranging from welfare to prisons and from health care to electricity rates. Deregulation, privatization, contracting out governmental services to the private sector, greater resort to various public/private partnerships to carry out a variety of public-oriented tasks and other such reforms are not just the results of a swing of the regulatory pendulum from liberal to conservative. Nor are such changes a return to a simpler, pre–New Deal time, when the role of the federal government was essentially minimal, in comparison with the present. Rather, changes now occurring in what may seem to be the margins of regulation are, in fact, central—they are defining new conceptions of the respective roles of the state and the private sector.

This shift from a national to an increasingly integrated global economy is as transformative for governance purposes as was the shift from a local to a national economy during the New Deal. Some of the effects of globalization, including a growing democracy deficit and new forms of state sovereignty, require a reconceptualization of the way we approach governance if such basic goals as citizen participation, fairness and transparency in decision making are to be attained.

Nowhere is the need for reconceptualization more immediately visible than in the new ambiguities of the public/private distinction. The public/private distinction once demarcated two relatively separate worlds—government and the private market.[2] Private capital markets tended to be primarily local, and capital had little mobility.[3] Private in this sense, however, has long passed into history. Moreover, deregulation and the various other regulatory reforms enacted to increase the efficiency of administrative agencies and regulation have merged the public and the private in various ways, often utilizing what previously were primarily private market approaches, techniques, and structures to advance public interest goals.[4] Given the dynamic aspects of the globalizing state, and the fact that the state is both an agent of globalization as well as an agent transformed by the processes of globalization, it is important to understand fully the global implications of these various deregulatory reforms at the legislative, administrative agency, and judicial levels. Public and private no longer mean the same thing and the legal approaches to these distinctions and the structures of governance that result from various new public/private partnerships need to change accordingly.

In this paper, I will articulate three areas of law influenced by globalization—and requiring a reconceptualization. As I will argue, new approaches to law should include those that focus more on the uses of power and their impact on citizens and less on who exercises that power, i.e., whether the entities involved are, technically speaking, public or private. Also, as government devises new ways to carry out its duties, after partnering with or delegating to the private sector, constitutional issues are likely to arise. Accordingly, I also advocate approaches to constitutional interpretation that emphasize flexibility, change, and a conception of state sovereignty that maximizes the opportunity of lawmakers to involve the state in new and creative ways.

THE GLOBAL REGULATORY DISCOURSE

Before examining the legal changes now occurring and those I believe that are possible, let me briefly explain more fully the way I am using the term "globalization." I then want to examine two different contexts of globalization and three different views on the impact of global processes.

As I use the term, globalization refers to a multiplicity of extraterritorial activities and their local effects. Specifically, it refers to complex, dynamic legal, economic, and social processes within an integrated whole, across territorial boundaries, often without the direct agency of the state. Globalization processes involve multidirectional flows—flows of ideas, images, goods, services, and people, and the communications networks necessary to sustain these flows.[5] What drives them, however, often has little to do with states directly. The social and economic forces that determine where and how, for example, capital might flow or labor markets develop are increasingly denationalized. This does not mean that states have no role to play, but even when they are involved, they are rarely in a position of autonomous power. They must usually cooperate with other states. Most often, transnational decisions are made without the agency of the state and without a prior determination of the *national* interest involved. Systems of law—many of them voluntary—have arisen to fulfill global as opposed to national interests in this sense. Domestic law itself is affected by denationalized systems of law, now developing voluntarily at the international level. The same also holds in the reverse. Increasingly, domestic regulatory approaches must take this global context into account if they are to be effective. The relationship of domestic law to globalization may come from various legal attempts to encourage or facilitate global processes or, on the other hand, attempts to resist them.

To get at the relationship of domestic law to global processes, I will focus on two aspects of globalization and law: (1) attempts on the part of the legal system to facilitate global processes and (2) attempts—through law—to resist global processes.

Encouraging Globalization

Those who seek to encourage globalization often speak of the "globalization of" markets, of law, of culture, etc. Used in this sense, globalization often implies uniformity, or homogeneity of laws or markets. It suggests, for example, that there are certain products, ideas, or legal provisions that can be marketed or adapted everywhere—on a global basis. This has a one-size-fits-all premise built into it. This view of globalization can also include the argument that globalization is, in effect, a form of Americanization or Westernization. The same is often said of markets—i.e., that they too are essentially Western in nature. Most important of all, this view of globalization implies a concept of linearity—i.e., these processes are progressing almost relentlessly toward a global market and a high degree of uniformity in laws, culture, and the economy. Under such a conception of globalization, the role of the state often merges with markets. Neoliberal reforms often are very much of a piece with this view of globalization. Indeed, some policies that further the goals of markets are affirmatively sought by some states, either in an attempt to extend the markets of their own constituents or to attract more investment to their respective jurisdictions. There also often is a sense of inevitability attached to this view of globalization, as if the inexorable process of the market is not or cannot be denied. At the extreme, such views of globalization suggest a substantial diminishment of the role of states and state sovereignty in particular. Indeed, some commentators have gone so far as to decree the processes of globalization as the cumulation of "the end of history."[6]

For many who hold such views, *laissez-faire* economics and governance thus coincide. Markets are given preference to states and the state's role, if any, is to ensure that markets can develop and thrive. In this mind set, the focus is on global competition and the limits of state action. Indeed, competition rather than cooperation is at the basis of approaches to global governance.

Resisting Globalization

Another set of reactions to globalization, however, focuses on resistance to global processes. Such approaches assume that global processes can be shaped or influenced by domestic law, if not stopped completely. This does not mean that markets, or market processes and approaches to regulation do not feature prominently in regulatory schemes, but decisions by lawmakers to opt for the market are not necessarily intended to equate globalization with *laissez-faire* economics. The market is used as a regulatory tool; it is not treated as a force of nature. Moreover, there may be many instances when market based responses are rejected outright.

Laws that resist globalization highlight the limits of globalization or at least the political limits of acceptance of global processes. Some skeptics of globalization believe that national law can effectively stop the negative impact of certain global processes on particular groups. Protectionist trade legislation is exemplary of a legal response along these lines. Other legal responses, however, represent opportunities for shaping global forces as they interact with local, domestic legal regimes. Whether one approaches globalization as a set of processes that can be influenced or resisted by national law results in a view of globalization that is not linear in nature. There is nothing inevitable about these processes or their outcomes. Indeed, in this sense, global processes can create transformative opportunities for domestic law. The domestic law that results is not in any way pre-ordained or inevitable.

Despite the attempts of some skeptics to wall out global forces entirely, it is not possible simply to assume that law can prevent global change and maintain the status quo. Global forces merge the global and the local into one modality, and how various communities—legal and civil society—react to these new possibilities is, to a large extent, up to them. Thus, as public functions move to the private sector and jurisdictions compete for investment and the jobs and economic development that accompanies investment, how individual legal regimes react is a major factor in how these trends are encouraged, modified, or controlled.

From these two points of view—facilitating global processes and resisting them—at least three perspectives on law and the literature on globalization emerge. As David Held has observed, there are hyperglobalists, skeptics, and transformationalists. Hyperglobalists see globalization as inevitable and the market forces unleashed by globalization as trumping political forces. The processes lead to linear change, culminating in various degrees of uniformity. The role of law is to facilitate global processes and the markets necessary for these processes to thrive. Markets trump law in terms of how outcomes are to be achieved.

A second school of thought is represented by the skeptics who often see globalization as a series of forces to be resisted and, in the event, as essentially regional in nature. From the law's point of view, it is the transnational aspect of these issues that makes them global whether or not we are dealing with the entire globe or only a portion of it. Nevertheless, this school of thought tends to see law more as a tool for resisting globalization in than facilitating it.

Finally, a third aspect of the global literature can be characterized as transformationalist in nature. Transformationalists see global processes as neither inevitable nor linear in nature. Rather, they are strong forces—economic, cultural, political—that can be shaped, influenced, and transformed, if you will, to suit local needs. The role of law in this context is one that sometimes tries to facilitate global processes, and sometimes tries to resist them. This approach to globalization is perhaps best captured by the word "cope." How can these global processes be transformed in ways that enable local economies to cope with these forces and, if possible, to thrive by successfully integrating them into or regulating them effectively?

LEGAL APPROACHES

It is with these three perspectives in mind that I wish to highlight three areas of law that, I believe, are crucial for transforming global processes in ways that minimize the democracy deficit and destructive aspects of global competition. One is at the international level. The other two areas of law are at the domestic level. At that level, one is statutory and the other constitutional. I begin with international or what might more accurately be called cosmopolitan law.

Cosmopolitan Law

By cosmopolitan law I mean law that is made by states, but law that nevertheless transcends any particular national interest so as to address a problem of global proportions. As David Held has defined it:

> By cosmopolitan law, or global law, or global humanitarian law, is meant a domain of law different in kind from the law of sates and the law made between one state and another for the mutual enhancement of their geopolitical interests . . . Cosmopolitan law refers here to those elements of law—albeit created by states—which create powers and constraints, and rights and duties, which transcend the claims of nation-states and which have far-reaching national consequences. Elements of such law define and seek to protect basic humanitarian values which can come into conflict, and sometimes contradiction, with national laws. These values set down basic standards or boundaries which no political agent, whether a representative of a government or state, should in principle, be able to cross.[7]

Human rights, the law of warfare, the Montreal Protocol on the Protection of the Ozone Layer are examples of this kind of law. Thus, one legal approach to the problems of global industries and global technologies that cut across numerous jurisdictions simultaneously is to try to legislate from above and impose a new layer of law at the top or, in this case, at the international level. It is, essentially, a hierarchical state-centered approach to law, yet it has its place and helps create a body of cosmopolitan law that can address multi-jurisdictional problems in a coherent way.

Another aspect of this world-government type of approach is the creation of international organizations such as the World Trade Organization (WTO), new bureaucratic entities developed to adjudicate and implement cosmopolitan law. As the Seattle demonstrations showed, there are important process issues involved in how such international organizations formulate and then enforce their policies. These issues include questions of transparency, participation, and fairness. The administrative law aspects of these processes are crucial to the resolution of these issues. I shall not deal with them in this paper, but they raise the question of the extent to which international administrative processes should be subject to a form of judicialization, one that is quite American in nature.

Another way of looking at this emphasizes the denationalized aspects of the policymaking that is occurring, especially at the informal or non-state level. As Jost Delbruck has argued:

> Today's financial markets are globalizing rather than internationalizing (which they did in earlier decades) since, for instance, the movement of capital has largely become independent of the sovereign control of state agencies. Thus, it seems globalization as distinct from internationalization denotes *a process of denationalization of clusters of political, economic and social activities.*[8]

As these companies become denationalized, so too does the law that governs them. Perhaps the primary example of such denationalized law is the extensive development of arbitration proceedings seeking to resolve disputes between companies doing business transnationally. These processes may depend on the legal preconceptions brought to bear on a problem by the arbitrator involved. Nevertheless, the primary orientation to such issues is, essentially, denationalized. There are, thus, wholly denationalized or privatized cosmopolitan legal systems developing through the voluntary regulatory regimes established by transnational corporations. International arbitration or a form of lex mercatori are examples of this. Their relationship to democracy and to domestic law are important issues and the procedures used even voluntarily are not beyond dispute. Of particular importance are the legal assumptions or legal baggage, if you will, of the arbitrator themselves. Depending upon their legal backgrounds and training, they often approach these proceedings differently. I shall, however focus my attention on the domestic level.

The Administrative Procedures Act

Four years ago, the Administrative Procedures Act (APA) turned 50. There were many symposia marking this milestone and various reforms and amendments to the Act were suggested.[9] The most common reform advocated was to include some form of cost-benefit analysis in the APA. Some of these cost-benefit reforms seek not only to maintain necessary regulation, but also to ensure that also the efficiency or regulation.[10] Other reforms define costs and benefits in ways that substantially limit the creation of any new regulations, often by utilizing complex procedures to make new rules impossible in anything remotely resembling a timely fashion.[11] This view has aptly been described as a form of "paralysis by analysis."[12] For the most part, however, a patchwork quilt of cost-benefit and risk-benefit approaches has been developing as individual statutes have incorporated their own versions of cost-benefit reform for the particular regulatory program involved.[13]

It may seem that this is a kind of progress—staving off the deregulators with reforms designed to make government "work better and cost less," in the words of the *Gore Report*. [14] Yet, in many ways it is a continuation of a long-standing debate in American administrative law between government intervention into the market and a relatively *laissez faire* approach to the economy. The words "cost" and "benefit" are capable of interpretations that allow for this age-old debate to continue, albeit in a slightly new form. Thus, the 104th Congress's proposals for cost-benefit reform would, if passed, have represented a form of procedural *laissez faire-ism* by requiring so much procedure that a kind of prospective deregulation would have occurred to all those agencies to which it applied.[15] A softer view of costs and a more flexible approach to benefit would allow government to proceed, albeit cautiously, largely as before.

There are a number reasons why economically based reforms have such saliency today. Global competitiveness concerns can reinforce ideological preferences for minimalist government—especially when one talks of federal regulation of various aspects of the economy and the environment. But quite apart from politics or ideology there are the very real economic limits for governments when low tax policies have been in effect for a significant period of time. Cost considerations are not limited solely to costs incurred by the regulated. Government costs also rise, and agency budgets decline, making new, cost-effective ways to achieve public interest ends increasingly important. To finance themselves, some agencies have resorted to new and extensive fee structures.[16] Other reforms have involved the creation of procedures designed to limit litigation by reaching a true consensus on a rule in the process of formulation.[17] Still others have sought to delegate their responsibilities to the market in the form of deregulation or to contract out certain responsibilities to various private actors.[18]

There are limits to the extent to which we can view citizens as customers and agencies as businesses. Whether these reforms further the "cost-benefit" state or the "administrative" state,[19] such approaches—based primarily on a state-centered approach—in my view, fail to take into account the dynamic global context described above and within which domestic public law reform is properly considered.

Rather than just focusing on making administrative law more efficient, I advocate changing the focus of domestic, regulatory law reform. From a global perspective, more pressing reforms are now in order. The more traditional roles of administrative law remain crucial: ensuring fairness, public participation and transparency in the resolution of disputes, and the creation of public policy. Without denying that sensible cost-effective reforms are important, I maintain that economics alone will not adequately provide the basis for global governance that will successfully integrate distinctive domestic legal approaches with international and global approaches to global issues. Nor will an economic discourse alone provide the tools necessary for linking legal structures in ways that increase the possibility for cooperative approaches to global issues, rather than unitary competitive responses. Let us turn, then, to what lies beyond economics in the transformation of public/private partnerships.

The APA and Public-Private Partnerships

The globalizing state is a decentered state and as much, it can no longer deal with many of today's concerns by exercising power in a monopolistic manner—in the old way. From a global point of view, it often may need to share power with other states more fully, and in certain proceedings, to incorporate these approaches into issues devised by nongovernmental entities whose range of influence and concerns transcend any single jurisdiction and whose perspectives and influence are global in scope. This may take the form of recognizing that certain domestic laws need to be harmonized with other states' laws or with international law strategies, thereby avoiding unnecessary regulatory competition and a race to the bottom. On other occasions, cost and regulatory effectiveness may mandate the creative use of market incentives to carry out tasks governments no longer can do or do as well. But were lawmakers to allow only a narrow economic sense of global competitiveness to drive these reforms as well as a view of the private sector that fails to understand the new partnerships the globalized state must now create, democracy would suffer. This is because the kind of democracy deficit we are talking about is not just the old debate between judicial and legislative decisionmakers. In these well-known public law debates, the democratic consequences of judicial decision-making are contrasted with those of elected legislators. But the global democracy deficit usually involves a much more stark comparison, between some public processes and none at all, when public/private is construed to take issues out of the public arena, democracy is left out completely.

Accordingly, I advocate three reforms of the APA. First, policymakers should extend its coverage to private entities carrying out essentially public duties. In other words, the APA should cover more than just governmental agencies. This is clearly shown in the context of FOIA reform. Second, the APA should devise procedures that open up the processes of contracting out public duties to private entities. Third, I believe that there should be a requirement in all rulemaking proceedings that the international and global implications of a proposed policy be considered explicitly—a kind of global impact statement, if you will. The National Environmental Policy Act (NEPA) required environmental impact statements;[20] we should require global impact statements as well. The premises behind all of these reforms are (1) that the public/private divide no longer satisfies the need for when process is necessary and when it is not and (2) local and global are now one modality.

Contracting Out

The informal rulemaking proceedings in Section 553 of the APA are elegantly simple.[21] They provide for notice and comment. A decision to contract out governmental services may not even be covered by these rulemaking provisions,[22] but even if it is, the provisions of a contract between a government agency and a private provider of services are not likely to be considered fully. This is especially true if the policy decision to contract out, not necessarily the details of the contract. Even if the details are noticed, its day-to-day implementation may not be visible to the public. The market logic of this approach is that you give certain responsibilities to private providers and review the bottom line only every few years or so, when the contract comes up for renewal. This increases the efficiency of the private providers and impresses upon them that whatever their tasks are whichever ones they agree and that these are their responsibilities and their responsibilities and theirs alone. But efficiency need not be the only goal. Moreover, such an approach assumes a distinction between administration and policymaking that does not exist in reality.[23] The process of administration inevitably involves policymaking, especially when emergencies or unusual circumstances arise. Thus, noticing the full details of a proposed contract with a private provider should be a minimum requirement of the privatizing process, but these contracts themselves may need to be subject to frequent review. Levels of accountability should be higher than those of normal market transactions, and contract renewals should be required every three to five years.

The Freedom of Information Act

Closely related to this reform is the fact that Freedm of Information Act (FOIA) should not be easily avoided just because certain public functions have now been contracted out. When private companies take over prisons, aspects of welfare screening, education, or city services such as snow or garbage removal, records created through the performance of a public duty that clearly would have been subject to FOIA if done by a governmental agency can now become private records, solely by virtue of the contractor's non-governmental status. As one report recently noted:

Without predictable judicial or legislative standards, the public risks being shut out of the privatization process. Without public awareness, public oversight of the operation of privatized governmental operations will be inadequate. It is clear that public access often suffers once governmental operations are turned over to private entities. Private enterprises serve managers, owners and shareholders, not taxpayers. According to fundamental democratic principles, governmental services conducted by private operators should be just as accountable as services provided by public agencies. The public and the press must be able to scrutinize the activities of private actors performing governmental services, just as the public and the press already scrutinizes public activities under public records statutes.[24]

Revising FOIA to take into account the role of the market and various forms of deregulation and privatization, today is necessary if the broad citizenship goals of this act are to remain within reach. When citizens are clients, they do not necessarily lose their need for information, though the essential nature of a private enterprise makes it, initially at least, focused more on profits and the stockholders than on providing information to taxpayers. At a minimum, the statute should be amended to include all private entities to whom public functions have been contracted.[25] Clearly, these are instances in which the mere label of "private" can result in cutting off information that clearly would "not be in the public interest.

A Global Impact Statement

More fundamentally, however, the administrative rulemaking process should include an explicit direction to consider seriously the global implications of proposed rules. This would not only encourage parties to the proceeding to present their perspectives on these matters, but also impress upon the decisionmakers involved that they are part of a complex national, international, and denationalized set of processes. Not all issues can be resolved in any one proceeding, but effective policymaking requires at least the consideration of the global implications of the rules involved. If, for example, stringent environmental regulations will shut down certain industries and move them offshore, what impact is this likely to have on global pollution? Are we to be the beneficiaries of this pollution by then being allowed to buy these imported goods at a lower cost than if they were produced here while others bear the pollution costs, but we enjoy the cheaper goods? Are there or should there be international efforts undertaken to try to achieve limits on certain pollutants that are global in nature? What efforts are underway? Will they be initiated? Such questions can help create a global discourse and a debate on the global public interests related to domestic regulatory proposals. Requiring they be explicitly considered by the agency involved may not only facilitate global preconditions for the creation of public policy that is meaningful on the global level.

CONCLUSION—A GLOBAL CONSTITUTION

Public/private partnerships, privatization, and the various new roles that the state is assuming can raise constitutional questions. The global constitution or, in effect, the domestic constitution seen through a global lens needs, in my view, to be a flexible one, one that can continue the long tradition in this country of adaptability when it comes especially to non-textual, structural constitutional principles such as federalism and separation of powers. That does not appear to be the direction of the current US Supreme Court, at least as it pertains to federalism. Chief Justice Rehnquist now speaks for a majority on the Court whose approaches to federalism issues are more open to arguments involving state autonomy and rejecting expansive reading of the Commerce Clause. Specifically, the Court takes issue with attempts by the federal government to "commandeer" state bureaucracies to carry out federal mandates.[26] Moreover, the Court attempts to breathe new meaning into the Tenth Amendment by arguing, for example, that federal regulation of guns near schools is too local an issue to be supported by the Commerce Clause of the Constitution.[27]

While a good doctrinal argument can be made in support of the Court's decisions in some of these cases,[28] their reasoning suggests a shift in the Court's methodology to such issues as well as an underlying philosophical approach to federal-state issues that transcends the facts of these cases. This shift in emphasis from federal power to state autonomy and power coincides with economic and political shifts in the global economy that also encourage decentralization of power. However, interpreting these changing in federal-state relations in a manner that diminishes the experimental flexibility of federal and state policymakers and new regulatory approaches runs the risk of substantially undermining the range of policy alternatives and administrative structures necessary for the global state to be effective.[29] This is because the changing rules of government and the private sector will require not only experimentation, but a fluidity in the exercise of power in today's contexts.

When choices of interpretive approaches to constitutional doctrines exist, those approaches that preserve, increase, or further the flexibility of decisionmakers' responses to global economy should be preferred. Not unlike the New Deal era when the Court had to confront new issues arising from society's political responses to a newly emerging nationally integrated economy, the Court today decides issues against a backdrop of an increasingly integrated global economy. A full analysis of the public/private distinction and recent federalism decisions would show that it is important for courts to resist constitutional approaches that unnecessarily limit change or new approaches to power-sharing. While it may seem ironic, some of the deferential, constitutional interpretive approaches forged by the Court during the New Deal era may, in fact, be best suited for the political experimentation that is now necessary, especially if government and non-state actors are to adapt successfully to the realities of a global economy. As I said earlier, however, this position does not imply we have returned to the New Deal—nor is it an argument for a return to the New Deal so far as substance is concerned. There is no going back to the nineteenth or twentieth century or to the state-centric future that courts and lawmakers have envisioned for the greater part of this nation's history.

NOTES

[1]Portions of this paper will draw heavily on some of my previously published work in: Alfred C. Aman Jr., "Proposals for Reforming the Administrative Procedure Act: Globalization, Democracy and the Furtherance of a.Global Public Interest," *6 Indiana J. Global Legal Studies 397* (1999) and Alfred C. Aman Jr., "The Globalizing State: A Future-Oriented Perspective on the Public/ Private Distinction, Federalism and Democracy," *31 Vand. J. Trans'l L.*, 769 (1998).

[2]See Sassen, *The Mobility of Labor and Capital*, supra note 7.

[3]Id.

[4]See Aman, *Administrative Law in a Global Era*, supra note 5, at 42–62.

[5]See generally, Appadurai Arjun, *Modernity at Large*, University of Minnesota Press (1996), p. 237.

[6]Fukuyama, *The End of History and the Last Man*, Hamish Hamilton (1992), p. 113.

[7]David Held, *Global Transformations*, 70 (1999).

[8]Jost Delbruck, "Globalization of Law, Politics, and Markets—Implications for Domestic Law—A European Perspective," *1 Ind. J. Global Legal Stud.* 9, 10–11 (1993) (emphasis added).

[9]Thomas O. McGarity, "The Expanded Debate Over the Future of the Regulatory State," *63 U. Chi. L. Rev.*, 1463, 1484–1527 (1996).

[10]Thomas O. McGarity, "A Cost-Benefit State," 50 Admin. L. Rev. 7, 38 (1998).

[11]Id. at 50.

[12]Id.

[13]Id. at 75.

[14]Al Gore, *National Performance Review, from Red Tape to Results: Creating a Government that Works Better & Costs Less* (Sept. 7, 1993).

[15]See generally, Paul Verkuil, "The Emerging Concept of Administrative Procedure," *78 Col. L. Rev.* 258 (1978).

[16]Alfred C. Aman, "A Global Perspective on Current Regulatory Reforms: Rejection, Relocation, or Reinvention?", *2 Ind. J. Global Legal Stud.* 429, 459 (1995).

[17]Id. at 455.

[18]Id. at 442.

[19]Id.

[20]National Environmental Policy Act of 1969, 42 USC. ' 4332(2)(c)(1994).

[21]Administrative Procedure Act of 1946, 5 USC. ' 553 (1996).

[22]Section 553 of the APA provides exemptions from its general rulemaking procedures. Among these is one granted for "matter [s] relating to . . . contracts." 5 USC. § 553(a)(2). This exemption has, however, generally been construed narrowly by the courts.

[23]Mark Aronson, "A Public Lawyer's Responses to Privatisation and Outsourcing," *The Province of Administrative Law* 40, 56-58 (Michael Taggart ed., 1997).

[24]Matthew D. Bunker and Charles N. Davis, *Privatized Government Functions and Freedom of Information: Public Accountability in an Age of Private Governance*, p. 25 (paper on file with author).

[25]TBA

[26]See, e.g., New York v. US, 505 US 144 (1992); Gregory v. Ashcroft, 501 US 452 (1991).

[27]US v. Lopez, 514 US 549 (1995).

[28]See Barry Friedman, "Federalism's Future in the Global Village," *47 Vand. L. Rev.* 1441 (1994) (arguing that the Court reinstate state sovereignty in New York v. United States).

[29]For a discussion of federalism advocating an alternate view—i.e., that federalism is an empowerment of the national government—see Erwin Chermerinsky, "The Values of Federalism," *47 Fla. L. Rev.* 499, 504 91995) (" [I] t is desirable to have multiple levels of government all with the capability of dealing with the countless social problems that face the United States as it enters the 21st century.").

Chapter 3:

REACHING OUT TO REGIONAL GOVERNMENT IN ENGLAND?

Kenneth Spencer
School of Public Policy, The University of Birmingham, UK

INTRODUCTION

The United Kingdom has undergone a transformation in both governmental and administrative reform within the regions of the country. Further devolution to Scotland, Wales, and Northern Ireland has taken place. Scotland now has its Parliament dealing with home affairs and able to create primary legislation. The previous Scottish Parliament "was adjourned, never to meet again, on 25 March 1707" (Black 2000: p. 1). Wales and Northern Ireland have their Assemblies, the latter in abeyance subject to further negotiations, responsible for home affairs matters though unable to create new primary statutes though able to comment upon and interpret legislation with a regional voice. The Scots Parliament and the assemblies came into being in 1999, with the Northern Ireland Assembly having a rather one-off early life and linked to cross border initiatives with the Irish Republic. In London, the mayor was elected on 4 May 2000, as were 25 members of the new Greater London Authority. The mayor, Ken Livingstone, the former Labour Member of Parliament turned independent, and the Greater London Authority took over running many aspects of Greater London on 3 July 2000.

In the other English regions there have been significant changes in relation to new integrated government regional offices, introduced in 1994, together with their subsequent adaptation since then. The English regions, some nine in total, have had, through legislation, new institutions added. The regional development agencies, essentially new non-government agencies dealing with economic regeneration and broader physical and social regeneration, were created in 1999. Similarly in the same year regional chambers, partnerships of business representatives with local government, voluntary sector and other regional stakeholders were created and have the right to be consulted by the Rregional development Agencies. In a number of English regions Regional Assemblies of indirectly elected local government politicians have been created by the regional local government associations.

In the case of London the regional development agency will be accountable to the new mayor of London and not to Parliament through the secretary of state for the environment, transport and the regions as in the other English regions. The London regional development agency also came into being following the Greater London Authority elections of May and was set up in the summer of 2000.

England, as well as the rest of the United Kingdom, has therefore undergone a major regional transformation of government and administration—the most significant for centuries. These changes in England are the focus of this paper. The outcomes of the current pattern of regional institutions and the political pressures for regional government, especially amongst local Labour parties, will largely determine the new pattern of governance at regional level in England. Much of the internal debate in the English regions follows from the referenda and legislation dealing with new devolved powers to Scotland, Wales, Northern Ireland, and London itself. The political debate is itself full of questions and often contradictions (Chen and Wright 2000).

Central government's own strategy on the English regions is one of evolution, but with a strong message from the prime minister that regional government in England is still some way off yet, even if it were a desirable aspiration. Other political figures press the case more strongly. The United Kingdom has witnessed nothing less than a new constitutional settlement in the years 1999–2000.

A new campaign based on political arguments about regional democratic accountability has been launched—the Campaign for English Regions. The campaign publicity argues that English regions are being left behind compared with other parts of the United Kingdom, though in London's case there has already been elections for a directly elected assembly (part constituency-based, part list-based, on a proportional vote for different political parties). The campaign calls for more devolution to English regions and the election of regional governments in England. The campaign is backed by four regions in particular—the North East, Yorkshire and Humberside, the West Midlands and the North

West—all are more strongly Labour Party–supporting regions in England, (Campaign for the English Regions 2000). There is also strong backing from the Local Government Association's Information Unit (Dungey and Newman 2000), again built around the issue of supporting regional democracy. The debate has been entered—the end result remains unclear.

In this paper the focus lies upon England and the issue of regionalism within its nine regions. Many English regions are simply artificial regions delineated for regional government office purposes. It has to be remembered that the English have had a highly centralised state control since 1066. The paper charts the moves toward regionalism in England from the late 1980s. It builds upon research funded by the UK Economic and Social Research Council which examined the issues surrounding the transformation of English regional government offices, (Spencer and Mawson, 1997, 1998a, 2000; Mawson and Spencer, 1997). This research developed our knowledge base of a neglected field of study in UK public policy. The previous key work dated from 1982 (Young 1982).

This paper is written at a critical time in the constitutional development of UK government and governance. An understanding of the evolution of the debate and the new regional institutions in England lies at the heart of this paper. It argues that the present position is one of confusion and greater regional fragmentation. It also reflects a lack of willingness on the part of central government to really tackle the key issue of modernising itself to more effectively deliver joined-up holistic policies regionally. The present position is one witnessing a plethora of new initiatives usually driven by single government ministers and their departments, often reflecting notions of an experimenting state. The drive and responsibility for English regionalism rests with the deputy prime minister and his ministers in the Department of the Environment, Transport, and the Regions (DETR).

The paper addresses the beginnings of the creation of the new integrated regional government offices in 1994 and concludes with the positive review of the roles of such regional government offices undertaken by the cabinet office in 1999 and 2000.

THE CREATION OF THE INTEGRATED REGIONAL GOVERNMENT OFFICES

New regional government offices began life on 1 April 1994. The then–Conservative government saw the key roles as identifying regional economic problems, improving economic competitiveness, enhancing regeneration capacity and ensuring more appropriate sustainability. The aim was to develop partnerships with regional stakeholders, for coordinated policy solutions. The initiative built upon some integration of the four initiating government department's policy programmes (employment, environment, industry and transport). Government offices were also expected to achieve the following (Government Offices Coordination Unit 1995: pp. 8–9): (1) securing coordination between parent government departmental programmes in their region, (2) an "eyes and ears" function to provide reliable information about regional issues and opinionsand (3) support for ministers in dealing with parliamentary business with a regional aspect.

The original ten government offices for the regions (GOs) of 1994 were created in response to the 1992 Conservative Party manifesto wanting to strengthen the coordination of government programmes and policies within regions. The manifesto called for a regional integration of appropriate Whitehall departments so that the business community and local government would have one port of call rather than several (Conservative Party 1992). The initiative was a key element of the enlivened debate on regional matters. It remains a factor in the current devolution debates, following the push by the Labour Government, elected in 1997, toward Scottish and Welsh devolution and change in Northern Ireland—all of which are now in place. Regional government within England has been and remains a growing political issue (Coulson 1990; Stoker, Hogwood, and Bullman 1995; AMA 1995; Bradbury and Mawson 1997; Elcock and Keating 1998; Mawson 1996; Regional Policy Commission 1996; Dungey and Newman 1999, 2000; Spencer and Mawson 2000; Bentley and Gibney 2000).

Other political pressures led to strengthening GOs in the English regions. In 1989, a parliamentary select committee identified no serious territorial analysis of public expenditure and no consistent disaggregated public expenditure data on English regions. There was inadequate planning of interconnections between regional programmes and their outcomes (House of Commons 1989). Both the Audit Commission (1989) and the National Audit Office (1990) felt that regional coordination of government policies was ineffective. This was because the centralised and departmentalised nature of central government made it historically difficult to ensure effective policy coordination at urban and regional levels. It was seen, in part, as being due to the then separateness of existing government department offices at regional level in England. This compared with integrated offices, the Scottish Office and the Welsh Office, in Scotland and Wales, respectively. These regions, as in Northern Ireland, were represented in the UK government cabinet by their respective Regional Secretaries of State. English regions are not represented in this way, although they often have larger regional populations.

There was also growing concern over the inadequate interaction of governmental support mechanisms to business and employment. Business leaders had been concerned to pressure the government into getting its regional act together to improve business competitiveness (Bennett, Wicks, and McCoshan, 1994; Bennett 1995; Moore and Richardson 1989; Storey 1994). Much of this debate concerned the fragmentation of various business support functions amongst, for example, Training and Enterprise Councils, Confederation of British Industry, Chambers of Commerce, English Partnerships, Rural Development Commission, the economic development functions of local government, and a wide range of separate government programmes managed through separate departments of regional government offices. Essentially this policy field was seen to be far too fragmented with not enough cross-cutting policy analysis and joined-up government.

At the same time, greater pressures were being felt as a result of European Union regional strategies and business competitiveness in the wider European and global contexts (Coopers and Lybrand/BITC 1992; Jones and Keating 1995; Garside and Hebbert 1989; Hebbert 1989). The lack of a stronger English regional approach had been felt to reduce access to European funds as well as hindering the competitiveness of English regional economies (Baine, Bennington, and Russell 1992; Batley and Stoker 1990; John 1996; Roberts and Hart 1996; Wannop 1995). There was a feeling that England did not, at subnational level, play as effective a part as it might within the European Union. The establishment by the European Union of the Committee of the Regions (1994) added credibility to the need to develop a stronger, more coordinated regional governmental presence in England (Commission of the European Communities 1994). At the same time the European Union was seen, itself, to be pursuing a stronger regional emphasis *(Harvie, 1994)*. It was moving toward a Europe of regions.

These roles for GOs can be seen in the wider context of government's and Whitehall's recognitions of the need for a new more holistic or joined-up approach to governance at regional level (Spencer and Mawson 1998b, 2000). The new offices reflected, unlike their predecessors, the need for more integration in an increasingly fragmented world of both institutions and policies of governance. The new integrated offices were required to operate in partnership mode to ensure greater regional effectiveness, especially with business (Coulson 1997; Spencer and Kunz 1993). This included the need to build stronger horizontal, not just hierarchical, links in government and the need to incorporate a stronger bottom-up structure to counter balance the hitherto strong top-down framework. In short, it was recognised that regional organisational capacity needed strengthening (Lewis 1992; House of Commons 1995) and that this would require the involvement of many key regional agencies often working in partnership.

The changing nature of both local and regional governance, with its many players and different voices including many quangos, required orchestrating. Perhaps the GOs were also seen as a vehicle for improving elements of the central-local government relationship. Clearly the offices were initially, and to a slightly lesser degree subsequently, seen as developing the administrative/managerialist arms of Whitehall—they were not directly seen as avenues for greater political involvement and regional accountability (Regional Policy

Commission 1996; Mawson and Spencer 1997). However, with the advent of Scottish and Welsh devolution, a similar accountability debate is growing in English regions. Through regional chambers, regional assemblies, and through the regional development agencies several English regions wish to move toward further regional political accountability (Dungey and Newman 1999, 2000). Such shifts of emphasis will require to build on many of the existing strengths of the GOs (Mawson and Spencer 1995; Spencer and Mawson 2000).

There were pressures from the Treasury and from other government initiatives seeking greater efficiency within the civil service—e.g., Citizens' Charter 1987, Next Steps Initiative 1988, Market Testing 1991, and the creation of the Office for Public Service and Science 1994. One of the underlying philosophies was to use the territorial dimension of public policy as a mechanism for encouraging greater cohesion in overlapping policy fields. Political support for the new integrated GO approach came particularly from the then-Conservative deputy prime minister who was also the secretary of state for the environment. Thus the creation of new style GOs was largely driven by internal circumstances within government, particularly concerned with rationalisation, with regional competitiveness, and with stronger coordination, as well as business pressures and growing evidence from select committees and elsewhere that better regional cohesion of Whitehall's activities was now necessary. It has already been shown elsewhere how the wider historical context fits neatly with various attempts to develop regional dimensions to government in England (Mawson 1996, 1997).

LAUNCHING THE NEW REGIONAL GOVERNMENT OFFICES

The Conservative government announced in November 1993 that the new integrated GOs would be established on 1 April 1994. The then-Secretary of State for the environment indicated that GOs would "provide their customers with a more comprehensive and accessible service . . . meet the widespread demand for a single point of contact . . . bring service closer to the people they serve, simplify the government machinery and improve value for money" (Department of the Environment 1993a).

The aim was clearly an attempt to coordinate an increasingly fragmented central government organisational structure deemed to be less-than-effective for the delivery of many services at the regional level. Lessons were being learnt from the Welsh and Scottish regions that were seen as benefiting from improved coordinated territorial management, devolved regional departments, block budgets, and the ability to switch resources between budget heads and programmes. A government committee noted that the regional secretaries of state valued this discretion enormously as "it assists policy coordination and financial management . . . it permits substantive policy differences and adjustment of UK policy measures in the light of different traditions and circumstances" (House of Commons 1989: p. 2).

Such an integrated approach challenged traditional ways of working, both ministerally and in the civil service. Six key objectives were established for new GOs (Department of the Environment 1993b). These were:

- to meet the operational requirements of departments and ministers;
- to contribute local opinions and experience to the creation and communication of government policy;
- to promote a coherent approach to competitiveness, sustainable economic development and regeneration using public and private resources;
- to develop the skills of civil servants and methods of working to achieve these objectives and to demonstrate their success in doing so;
- to develop partnerships with and between all the local interests to promote and secure these objectives;
- to provide a single point of contact for local people and deliver high quality services to citizens' charter principles (a quality assurance scheme).

Other less publicised governmental objectives, unspecified above, were for GOs to get a firmer grip for central government on European funding, to cut the costs of the integrated GOs through staff reductions and, to launch in parallel, a new single regeneration budget (SRB) (Department of the Environment 1993c, 1993d). The SRB was to be managed by the new GOs. The programme drew together some 20 previously separate programmes from five government departments totalling some £1.4 billion in 1994/95. The purpose was one of providing flexible support for social and economic regeneration and well-being. It was available through a competitive bidding system managed by GOs. Thus a key initial task for the GOs was to ensure the smooth and successful operation of this new SRB programme, itself being a coordinated package of previously disparate programmes. Bids were invited from various agencies of governance in partnership with others and supported by local communities (Hogwood 1995; Mawson et al. 1994; Stewart 1994).

The SRB programme was central to the early life of GOs and considerable attention was given by regions and Whitehall to ensure its success. Indeed the very positive response by government to the management of SRB by GOs was instrumental in the Labour Government's build up to the creation of Regional Development Agencies (RDAs) in each of the nine English regions on 1 April 1999 (though the London RDA was to follow a little over one year later).

The original ten GOs were located in each of the following English regions: North East; North West; Yorkshire and Humberside; Merseyside (to be later integrated with the North West); West Midlands; East Midlands; Eastern Region; South West; South East; London. Regional civil servants of the Departments of Employment (in 1995 Education and Employment), Environment (in 1997 Environment, Transport and the Regions), Transport, and Industry, all became accountable in a new GO managerial structure to one senior regional director (later regional director). The regional director originally reported to all four secretaries of state and was accountable for all staff and resources routed through GOs and also responsible for establishing cohesive and effective coordination. Links with other government departments were also developed—e.g., Home Office; Culture, Media, and Sport (partly in relation to the voluntary sector and lottery funding); Defence (in relation to future use of military sites).

As part of the downsizing, or rightsizing, of the civil service a senior management review was undertaken. Two civil service white papers set out the approach. This review impinged upon the GOs almost as soon as they were beginning to find their feet. The white papers required these reviews to aim for "leaner, flatter management structures with less emphasis on working through hierarchies and more scope for talented individuals to make their mark" (Cabinet Office 1994, para. 4.15). The reviews were to prepare proposals for new senior management structures, including GOs, which would also "ensure that departments are organised to deliver the services they provide . . . as efficiently and effectively as possible; and to match the management structure to the needs of work, with clear lines of responsibility and accountability; and to reduce layers of management . . . based on a clear understanding of the added value of each layer of management" (Cabinet Office 1995, para. 4.7).

The outcome of the GO's review carried out by the government office central unit in Whitehall, was a reduction of some 32 percent of the senior posts in GOs (grades 2–6). One of the impacts of this review and of issues to do with integrating terms and conditions, office location, and personnel matters was to initially emphasise internal management issues in GOs at the expense of wider strategic considerations (Government Office for the Regions 1995). However, one result of the staff reductions was to further encourage cross-departmental working by senior managers across GOs activities simply because it was no longer possible to retain a very senior official in GOs from each of the four merging departments. The outcome was that GOs were reasonable well-placed structurally, at senior level, to consider cross-cutting or wicked issues, as well as develop coordinative mechanisms to assist more holistic joined-up government in the regions.

Despite GO's attempts to integrate a more coherent package of policies regionally there remain many relevant policy fields outside the scope of GOs whilst there remains disquiet over some of the regional boundaries and whether people relate to local regions or not (Hogwood 1996; Harding et al. 1996). In

England there is not generally strong historic affiliation to regions in any governmental sense.

MANAGING GOVERNMENT OFFICES

To oversee the GOs initiative at Whitehall level, a central management board was created. This was chaired, rotating regularly, by a senior Whitehall civil servant, grade 2 or 3. The board met with regional directors and was serviced by the government office central unit (GOCU), a unit staffed by seconded civil servants from departments launching the initiative. The board, in collaboration with regional directors, set overall objectives, with operational detail left at regional level. Most GOs were broadly similar in terms of functions (incorporating prior regional office functions plus new additions—e.g., SRB, European Funding, and lesser roles in education and safety). While many governmental and other functions lay outside the scope of the GOs, there was and is opportunity for informal influence. This can be quite powerful given the regional directors' networks of Whitehall and ministerial links. Regional directors are directly responsible to ministers and through them to Parliament. They are not accountable regionally to any political body—though the introduction of regional chambers and assemblies has meant that one of the tasks of regional directors has been to liaise with such bodies and keep them informed, as well as obtaining feedback for government from such bodies.

Regional directors occupy relatively powerful positions in the Whitehall machinery and their status has been growing as a result of their roles, activities and significance to Whitehall and to government. They often act as challengers of central uniformity. Whilst functions, management structures and relationships broadly follow common patterns found elsewhere in Whitehall there are several major differences reflected in GOs organisational structures and links with Parliament.

An important difference was that under the Conservatives the GO London serviced a cabinet sub-committee on London and had direct access by this route to all London-wide government and Whitehall key players. In London, the creation of the Greater London Authority and the election of Ken Livingstone as mayor, now means that from May 2000 the London GO will be responsible to the mayor of London (see later). Both GO London and GO Merseyside took over responsibilities for the now defunct urban development corporations, whilst the originally separate Merseyside GO inherited large scale Objective One European funding. Such funding is aimed at restructuring major declining industrial regions in Europe. Thus, GO emphasis on policy often centred on specific regional interests. The English rural interests were exemplified best by the Eastern Region and the South West. Both of these GOs were actively involved in preparing the rural white paper for example (due in 2000).

Internal GO management structures differed. In the South West there was a co-office located in Plymouth as well as the Bristol office and a sub-Office in St. Ives. This was essentially to reflect local politics. In the South East the management of the GO was organised geographically rather than functionally, with the early evidence indicating success as a regional managerial approach. The South East region surrounds the core London region and thus represents a hollowed doughnut shape. Both these regions often need to co-operate for effective policy development programmes.

In most GOs the original separate departmental functional structures were mixed at middle and senior management levels in order to assist integration and to help managers grow out of their historic departmental silos of thinking. It was a means of getting senior staff to think beyond the box. It was common for senior functional service managers in GOs to take on board some responsibilities for sub-regional geographical area coordination within the region. Such an approach also helped to break down departmental barriers and ensured regular contacts were made with local stakeholders and representative groups in these sub-regions. Such styles of management have proved effective in helping senior managers to develop a wider GO perspective. Over time, as GO civil servants return to Whitehall and as others move for a period into the GOs, the developing ethos of Whitehall's functional structures become more influenced by a territorial dimension of policy relevance to specific geographical regions and specific communities. This should, over the medium to longer term, contribute to more realistic and improved policy process management by Whitehall. It will sensitise civil servants more strongly to regional perspectives.

The roles of GOs as "eyes and ears" should not be underestimated. It is clear that GO regional directors and other senior staff, have been influential in challenging current thinking and in formulating policy and systems in Whitehall. There is still much progress to be made, but the regional dimension is now rolling in Whitehall. Indeed it can be argued that experience at senior management levels in GOs, alongside the new approaches to government thinking more holistically, places such regional civil servants at the cutting edge of cultural change and joined-up government within Whitehall itself. The cabinet office reviews of the roles of GOs, reporting in February 2000, has emphasised the key role that GOs can play in joined-up or holistic government, especially in relation to cross-cutting or wicked issues (Cabinet Office 2000).

There remain other links to be forged in effective management terms with GOs. The move toward the quango state and its fragmentation readily identifies some further prime concerns about holistic government—e.g., health bodies, housing corporation, higher and further education (Skelcher 1998). With a number of new government initiatives some of these linkages are now being forged—though sometimes on strong Whitehall departmentalist lines such as health action zones, education action zones, and employment action zones. Again, the cabinet office report of 2000 recognises the dangers inherent in such an approach of too many specific functional initiatives. The treasury has also become concerned at the costs and lack of linkages between such initiatives, as well as being concerned to see real evidence based analysis of programme impact.

In terms of GO budgets no regional dimension was build into negotiations between the Treasury and individual Departments of State. Thus GOs depended upon the delegation of elements of budgets from these central functional departments, each of which operated different financial management systems. These were usually poor in information technology terms. This led to difficulties of coherence and coordination at central level that had to be tackled regionally. At the same time regional director's own lines of accountability to several ministers could lead to tensions. Whitehall departments often took a defensive position in relation to GOs, particularly those outside the main sponsoring department of environment, transport and regions. The regional agenda was too often seen as an issue for this department, rather than a wider issue for government as a whole. This view is still strong within government.

The GOs were involved in annual bid rounds for resources from their various parent Departments. The link was GO-MINIS, a technical system linked to the annual public expenditure round. GOs prepared objectives and activities for the next year, which were negotiated with parent departments and with GOCU. Once approved, GO-MINIS documents were transformed into annual operational plans and budgets for specific divisions within each GO. This system also led through the operational plans into GO annual reports for ministers and for general public accountability. The 1998 change by the treasury to a three-year expenditure planning system, rather than the previous annual system, was able to create a little more certainty in the financial medium term for the regions.

The GOs established cross-office working groups linked to Whitehall staff (known as twinning) to examine regional issues in relation to a large number of policy areas. Some led to policy or priority changes—e.g., road proposals, regional airports, rural white paper, ministry of defence land, careers service, SRB, business link schemes, securing European social fund grants for government training programmes, encouraging investors in people quality standards, producing new regional planning guidance and developing analysis of regional economies. Via the twinning approach new networks were formed, new influences were placed on policy formulation and implementation. The voice of regional civil servants was being heard more and was slowly being acted upon.

Despite attempts to influence policy in Whitehall it is still the case that all too often the regional dimension is not considered appropriately or opportunely. Parent Whitehall departments as well as other departments often lacked understanding of the roles and opportunities presented by GOs. Clearly the GOs need a specific set of regional priorities, performance measures and guidelines in order to manage effectively. These are not always in place. GOs, do, however, have considerable discretion in the management and allocation of funding directed through their own offices. GOs are in a position to affect both inputs and outcomes of a variety of policy fields in both a formal and informal sense. Much of their real power base lies in their brokerage, funding, and informal influence roles.

There has been criticism of GOs aimed at regional directors having too much power, discretion, influence and choice in many policy areas and that there is too little scrutiny of their activities (Foster 1995). Such a position can emerge from the contradictions between varying perceptions of the nature of GOs and regional reform. Change brings critique, it also takes time to evolve and settle down. There have been successes to which regional directors can readily point (Ritchie 1996). Criticisms over regional accountability have been strong and the roles of regional development agencies, regional chambers, and regional assemblies have included some small moves in the direction of greater regional accountability, but it must be remembered that as civil servants regional directors remain responsible to Parliament.

In the light of all of this the House of Commons' trade and industry committee of 1995 was able to argue that regions needed a more proactive approach. It was also felt that they needed to foster enhanced organisational capacity across key regional stakeholders. This was to be achieved through preparing regional and sub-regional plans to co-ordinate activities across agencies. However, the then contradiction was that GOs, under the Conservatives, were not given that role partly because of a political dislike of regional planning. The new regional development agencies of 1999 have been an approach by the Labour Government, elected in 1997, to stimulate the shift back to regional economic planning, using the business community as a main driving force through non-governmental bodies—the regional development agencies.

The regional directors of GOs are expected to work with local authorities, the regional local authority association, other public agencies, the business community, regional development agencies, chambers, and assemblies and the voluntary sector (which incidentally is not normally structured or organised at regional level). There are specific tensions between on the one hand the role of representing government in the region and co-ordinating its service delivery and policies and, on the other hand, that of reflecting regional views back to Whitehall (which may be sensitive and highly critical).

The evidence indicates that it is easier for GOs to progress systems, procedures and structures in the region, often by encouraging others to play a leading role. Policy influence is Whitehall is slow to develop, though there have been a few relatively important successes. In some cases policy influence is wisely handled outside the formal decision-making structure. There is small, but growing, evidence that Whitehall civil servants have begun to acknowledge the regional dimension as sometimes an issue to be addressed in their own deliberations. The traditional cultures of Whitehall are shifting a little. The devolution debate and associated English regional chambers and assemblies as well as new regional development agencies are likely to continue to push for further change to long established Whitehall cultures. English regions could well become more central to the transformation of Whitehall itself. The struggle has been joined.

Certainly GOs work in a far more integrated way than ever before, though some are disappointed that GOs had not earlier opened up to more active involvement of local institutions in their work (Fell 1995; Association of District Councils 1995). Independent regional chambers and assemblies have been created in regions with strong local political representation. Such chambers and assemblies can be created in regions, which wish to establish them subject to agreement by the secretary of state for the environment, transport and the regions. These bodies are not the creatures of GOs but are independently connected. Regional development agencies operate with Boards of around seventy per cent business people. Thus the two key constituencies of criticism of their lack of involvement in regional matters, local government and business are finding themselves incorporated within the new developing aspects of GOs work. GOs are still an evolving feature of a new Whitehall approach to the English regions. They have the potential to act as significant elements in government networking and influence, as well as an arbitrator, with others, of regional concerns reflected back to Whitehall.

The Regional institutions are seen as crucial to economic strategy and to improving competitiveness. However gaining resources, other than from the department of environment, transport and the regions, still remains elusive through a treasury spending review in 2000 may shift the balance a little more in favour of the GOs integrated approaches to policy and its implementation.

GOs have, since 1994, represented a significant development in the machinery of government at regional level. Despite criticisms they are likely to evolve either as a growing powerful instrument of administrative decentralisation or potentially as a more regionally recognised form of devolved English regional democratic structure. Either way, the change is a significant constitutional shift from the pattern of Whitehall as we knew it (Hennessy 1989; Gray 1994; Rhodes 1997; Skelcher 1998). GOs in England can play a crucial role in further decentralised and devolved constitutional change with their enhanced capacity both administratively and politically.

SOME LESSONS FROM THE GOVERNMENT REGIONAL OFFICES

A number of key lessons and findings have emerged from the study of GOs. Briefly summarised they include the following:

- The transformation to a more holistic, joined-up, governance will need to build on the skills and knowledge of senior civil servants in the English regions. Regional directors could well be developing these skills most needed to provide twenty-first century government in England, which is both effective and integrated. Senior regional civil servants have been placed at the cutting edge of cultural change within Whitehall.

- There remains strong resistance in many parts of Whitehall to developing a policy focus for GOs, particularly beyond those government departments not formally involved in initiating GOs. Yet some of these departments are developing stronger links with GOs—e.g., Home Office; Culture; Media and Sport; Education and Employment; Defence and the Cabinet Office.

- GOs were highly successful in the coordination and management of new programmes that cut across traditional departmental boundaries, e.g., SRB, European funding, challenge funding schemes, competitiveness policy development.

- GOs relationships with local authorities, especially larger urban ones, and with other regional bodies, can be tense but are generally improving as networks and partnerships develop.

- GOs are seen by Whitehall as a coordinated regional administrative presence of government and also as a source of regional intelligence. Regionally they are seen as powerful, allocating significant resources and holding considerable discretion. Their regional directors are seen as not really accountable regionally.

- GOs have been used by the Labour Government as a vehicle in resurrecting regional development agencies. Much energy in 1998/99 was expended in this direction by GOs. The great danger is that this could detract from the very positive coordinative work that was being considerably enhanced across other key policy fields. The agencies may, however, give a clearer focus on the regional competitiveness agenda. The agencies are independent of GOs, In some respects they therefore add further to the fragmentation of regional governance.

- GOs have been successfully active in prompting new regional networks and partnerships in order to assist policy development and intra-regional cooperation. One danger is that in some regions a large number of new partnerships have been forged, again adding to fragmentation—especially where there are tensions and conflict between various stakeholders within and between partnerships.

- The traditional vertical organisational structures of Whitehall sit uneasily alongside a regionally, horizontal integrated approach. Twenty-first century government may require more of the latter rather than the former in dealing with fragmentation, the hollow state and in drawing wider participative interest in regional and sub-regional policy frameworks. Uniformity is giving way to discriminate tailored policy adaptation and an ability to tackle cross cutting issues. GOs can present a wider complementary opportunity for testing alternatives to existing Whitehall systems.

- GOs have enabled Whitehall to exercise a much firmer grip on the flow of European funding into the regions. Though the review of EU structural funds results in a smaller share for the UK as a whole from 2000.

- In their short lifespan thus far GOs have been able to operate in a more regionally integrated manner. They can be innovative and provide an embryo of challenge to current departmentalist perspectives in Whitehall. The need for joined up or corporate policies from Whitehall is strongly pressed by regional directors along with others, including those in the cabinet office.

THE CREATION OF REGIONAL CHAMBERS, ASSEMBLIES, AND REGIONAL DEVELOPMENT AGENCIES IN 1999

Regional chambers, assemblies and regional development agencies (RDAs) are new dimensions of the Labour Government's approach to English regional administration. These three distinct new elements to regional governance can be briefly outlined as follows. Regional development agencies were created by legislation in April 1999 (2000 in London). They are given the task of improving regional economic competitiveness. Each has a government appointed chair, usually a businessperson, who oversees a board of 12 members with six drawn from the business and commercial worlds. Other key agencies are represented on the board, including local authorities, the voluntary sector and other players, e.g., universities. The board is serviced by a chief executive and paid staff many of whom transferred from the relevant regional GOs, from the rural development commission and from English partnerships. The London RDA followed the formal creation of the new Greater London Authority on 3 July 2000.

Regional chambers can be created where the secretary of state for the department of the environment, transport and the regions agrees to designate a body as a regional chamber. Chambers are public-private partnerships. Chambers have a majority of local government indirectly elected councillors on them, but not more than seventy per cent of the membership. Others come from major regional stakeholder groups. The chamber is seen as a mechanism for local and regional concerns and as an element of accountability, as the RDAs are required to consult chambers in preparing their economic strategies. In the case of London the newly elected London Assembly with the newly elected Mayor will provide the key consultation-reporting link in a much more direct accountability structure.

Regional Assemblies are found in these regions where they have been established with all political party support. They bring together all the local authorities to provide a new non-statutory political regional level of local government organisation. Outside London they have not been directly elected but exist in a variety of forms, so that in some cases, e.g., North West Region, a separate assembly does not exist as it is integrated into the chamber. There is thus a degree of present confusion over terminology and the voluntary nature of these chambers and assemblies. Chambers and assemblies have few resources to build regional capacity. In the case of the London Assembly, elected in May 2000 and which became responsible for the Greater London Authority in July 2000, the position is much clearer with transparent responsibilities being set out.

The 1998 Regional Development Act set up the RDAs. In Wales, Scotland, and Northern Ireland and London the regional RDAs will be responsible to elected regional authorities and, in the first three, cases regional governments. Elsewhere these new RDA quangos are responsible to the secretary of state for the environment, transport and the regions who is also the deputy prime minister, and to a lesser degree, on consultation, to the new regional chambers (Shutt 2000).

The legislation sets out the roles which RDAs are expected to cover as:

- To further the economic development and regeneration of its area.
- To promote business efficiency, investment and competitiveness in its area.
- To promote employment in its area.
- To enhance the development and application of skills relevant to employment in its area.
- To contribute to the achievement of sustainable development in the UK where it is relevant to its area to do so (Regional Development Act 1998: Section 7[1]).

Each RDA was required to submit its first regional economic strategy to government by the end of 1999. This provided the base for future work. However, it is not clear from these strategies how they will be appropriately funded. In particular, the question remains how they will be able to draw on a wide variety of governmental department budgets outside the remit of the department of environment, transport and the regions—which is the initiating government department. In the summer of 2000 extra central funds were made available for RDAs but with strong pressure to make RDAs more effective in terms of positive impacts and outcomes on regional economies.

Against this background of new regional governance structures GOs are in a key position. GOs have an ability and potential to achieve the necessary coordination across these new Labour Government initiatives where they are enabled or allowed to play both formal and informal roles in networking, advice, decision-making and implementation.

A number of GO staff and functions were transferred to RDAs, mainly from Single Regeneration Budget roles and from these dealing with inward investment, innovation, technology transfer, and regional competitiveness. Despite this, RDAs only had limited primarily regeneration budgets from the DETR to work with in their first year. This was augmented in year two. Other government departments were less keen to provide their resources to be targeted at regional competitiveness. The Treasury Spending Review of 2000 has addressed this issue and is pressing for further integration. The current position clearly reflects the still serious lack of effective joined-up government by central government itself.

There are ambiguities built into the roles and responsibilities of chambers, assemblies, and RDAs. These can open opportunities for conflict and discord. RDAs are required to consider the views of properly constituted chambers, but they are not accountable to the chambers. RDAs can also consult independently with various stakeholder groups, including partnership networks in the region. The result could be that RDAs might play off one group of interests against another group. Certainly in the short term the GOs will need to assist the private sector led RDAs to develop their communication and political skills in the complex world of public and private sector interaction. There are some signs that discord amongst the various regional stakeholder groups can be disruptive and lessen impact (Ayres and Davis 2000). There are also signs of frustration at the lack of progress by RDAs in some regions.

How the various institutional roles develop in future will very much depend upon the skills of the regional directors, the chairs of chambers, and the chairs and chief executives of RDAs and the iterative role of assemblies. The scene is set for a more powerful regional interaction with Whitehall—an interaction to which Whitehall will inevitably have to respond. Such responses will press Whitehall to a more regionally responsive mode and add to the many pressures for further cultural change in Whitehall. Pressures for English regional budgets for a range of services could well emerge. This will inevitably mean Whitehall and government giving up some of its power—no doubt reluctantly. It will be too easy for government to give away other people's power—e.g. regional quangos, national agencies, local government. The pressures, however, on government itself to release some of its own power will not diminish. Only by doing so will joined-up government become a reality.

REVIEW OF THE ROLE OF GOVERNMENT OFFICES

Spencer and Mawson (2000) draw attention to the key point in the regional governance debate that the Labour Government in pressing its new RDA and chamber initiatives, mistakenly took its eye off the developing role of GOs. The danger was one of yet greater regional fragmentation. This is precisely what has happened. However, the government has in the light of criticism such as the above undertaken a review of the role and functions of GOs (Cabinet Office 2000). This review has also taken place against the background that GOs have strengthened the position of central government in the regions, rather than that they have either strengthened regional devolution or strengthened existing local government democratic institutions (Mawson and Spencer 1997).

Local government is pressing for greater regional democratic accountability (Dungey and Newman 2000). Yet whether this will really remain in the best interests of local government and its strengthening remains a questionable proposition. At the same time, the government's modernisation agenda is being pursued on a variety of fronts—e.g., Beacon Councils, Best Value, City Mayors, new styles of local government political structures including cabinet and scrutiny committees, new approaches to political leadership, the use of performance indicators, policy outcome emphasis and measurement, evidence based policy analysis and evaluation, plus partnership working with private and voluntary or not-for-profit sectors. This does raise the issue of how the regional governance debate demonstrates connections to the parallel ongoing modernisation agenda of the Labour Government. It also links to the "reinventing government" emphasis seeking the "plurality of providers and emphasising quality and consumer satisfaction" (Hill 2000: p. 87). One of the goals of government in relation to a new revival of local democracy is to enhance public involvement in decision making and to encourage greater voter interest through new governmental structures and positions—e.g., London mayor and Greater London assembly elections. The regional government agenda also sits alongside this debate.

At the same time government is building into a number of its priority programmes a regional role to sit between a central, national focus and a local, city, or sub-regional focus. Thus, in relation to the new Strategy for Neighbourhood Renewal, the executive summary is able to state that the idea of regional coordination is crucial. "The Performance and Innovation Unit's (PIU's) report, Reaching Out, argued for the strengthening of Government Offices for the Regions (GOs) to help join up regional activity. This has potential to assist neighbourhood renewal—working with Regional Development Agencies (RDAs)" (Cabinet Office 2000b: p. 9 para. 29).

The government's review of the role of the GOs highlights a number of key points (Cabinet Office 2000). Some of these are set out below; they can in part be seen to fall within the government's framework for modernising government at local and regional level with a clear emphasis on improving the coordination of public services as a priority.

The review is concerned that "Regional networks of Government Departments are fragmented with no part of central government responsible for bringing its contribution together to assist local areas. Problems are becoming more acute, and greater importance is attached to integrated solutions to local problems" (Cabinet Office 2000: p1). The proposed solution? "Strengthened and higher profile Government Offices are needed in the regions covering all Government policies affecting local areas, with more discretion on how to achieve results—but more clearly accountable for delivery of cross-cutting outcomes" (ibid. p. 1).

This new GO's role is expected to deliver through a series of initiatives. First, GOs will work closely with RDAs. Second, there will be strengthened ministerial and Whitehall coordination of policy initiatives and government offices. Third, more focus on strategic outcomes of government initiatives affecting local areas with clear success indicators. Fourth, the 2000 Treasury Spending Review has resulted in a greater link up amongst the multitude of different governmental department, area based, policy programmes.

The cabinet office review fails to address, in the short term, the development of elected regional government in England. "The proposals . . . should be robust against reasonable assumptions about elected regional government in England. They neither require nor preclude this . . . One effect of elected regional government could be to involve closer over-sight of regional agencies by the elected body. But this does not affect what needs to happen in the shorter term . . . More broadly, elected regional government is not likely to be introduced for some time. The changes proposed . . . should sensibly be introduced at an earlier stage" (Cabinet Office 2000: p. 9).

The review also recognises that changes regionally will also impact upon the nature of central government and the civil service. This issue is one not fully addressed previously and may be taken as a signal that central government and the civil service as a whole were not willing, or able to grasp the implications of the regionalism concept of fuller administration or wider devolution (Spencer and Mawson 2000). It is proposed that a new unit working on behalf of government as a whole, based in the cabinet office which supports the prime minister, would take over from the Government Offices Management Board, the Government Office Central Unit, and the Inter-department Support Unit for Area-Based Initiatives. Previous government departmental functions largely from DETR are thus proposed for incorporation and transfer to the prime minister's remit.

This new proposed central unit would manage GOs, improve coordination, and provide better collective consideration to change regional or local networks. At the same time, the 2000 Treasury Spending Review has rationalised area-based spending through a greater focus on outcomes, greater linkage between area based programmes, considering the possible pooling of budgets, even considering cross-cutting regional budgets. It is also proposed that new budget arrangements are needed to ensure better links between departmental, European structural funding, and lottery funding. The latter point will enable central government to have greater control over the strategic direction of national lottery funding. This has now grown in significance as a huge regional funder, but is currently independent of government and therefore of government strategic direction. Government aims to pull the lottery fund more in the direction of strategic regional funding and thus joined up funding streams.

A clear critique would be that many of these proposals lack teeth at the moment. There is no great will on the part of central government to go down the elected English regional government route. Though now that the Scots have a Parliament, the Welsh and Northern Irish their elected assemblies, there could be a strong case for an English wide Parliament or assembly in addition to the United Kingdom Parliament. Much may depend upon the outcome of the work of the Greater London Authority—as a model of what may be achieved elsewhere. Structural managerial change is a common governmental response to problems—of itself it rarely has the desired effect. The issue is really much more to do with the culture and attitudes of government departments, their ministers and the traditions of the civil service. These will need to change and there will need to be greater trust between ministers and departments to make for effective decentralised regional administration. It is difficult to see the current proposals propelling much significant change in the short term.

All this has led to the belief that the advent of the new GOs, RDAs, regional chambers, London assembly, regional assemblies are no more than a series of interesting governmental experiments. Thus the policy on English regionalism will evolve as part of the experimenting state structure. As a result this is likely to delay the introduction of elected regional government within England.

Perhaps why these experiments look like being over taken by the prime minister's office is both to ensure better coordination, but also, more significantly, to give the prime minister and cabinet office a greater degree of control over direction in a policy area that has become confused, led to greater fragmentation, and could provide significant local political pressures for change on grounds of regional accountability. The trigger for public pressure for accountability could come were taxation powers to be granted regionally. If this is seen as an extra tax burden it is likely to be resisted very strongly. There are no votes in introducing any form of regional taxation in England. The transfer of existing tax income sources to any regionally accountable body would obviously be more likely. However, outside the present devolved structures of Scotland and London, this power of devolved taxation to regional English level looks some time well into the future. Though the London model may result in similar structures being considered for the major urban areas of the UK, though this is likely to be at sub-regional level in other English regions.

CONCLUSION

In the transformation of government urgent reforms are called for, especially if democracy is not to be further eroded (Foster and Plowden 1996; Dungey and Newman 2000). The development of GOs provides a building block in this direction. Others have argued that systems of regional government in Europe are not as central to economic innovation and competitiveness as is sometimes assumed (Harding et al. 1996). However, it is clear that regional economic partnerships and networks, plus the advent of regional development agencies, are all regarded regionally as useful driving forces.

A further key element of potential learning and transformation would be for GOs to extend their role in dialogue with the wide variety of regional quangos (Skelcher 1998). The appointed state and its fragmentation can be drawn together at regional level probably more easily than centrally in Whitehall. There is scope for further development by GOs in this area. Though the varying levels of regional identity and some regional boundary issues still affect any populist move toward regional government.

Rhodes argues that "Institutional differentiation and disaggregation contradict command and control by bureaucracy. Thriving functional representation contradicts territorial representation through local governments. These contradictions are keys to understanding recurrent policy failures, even disasters" (Rhodes 1997: p. 199). However, an attempt to introduce a territorial dimension into English regional outposts of Whitehall through GOs, which to some degree are bound to go native, is one way of beginning to explore where contradictions and where complementarily fit within Whitehall. In this context the potential of GOs, building on their successes to date, can be very significant for the next century of English government and governance.

The growth of many partnerships, stimulated by GOs, themselves has added to the complexity of the regional tier of administration. Perhaps now is a time for some rationalisation and weeding out of ineffective bodies. The English regions do need to address the number function and balance of partnership for effective administration and governance.

GOs represent a key challenge to existing patterns of Whitehall working. Many, including those in Whitehall, recognise that there does need to be change. In the typical traditions of Whitehall such change is usually seen as evolutionary (Butler 1993). GOs fit this model. Such change is not before its time (Eser 1996; Spencer 1988; Spencer et al. 1986). They also have the potential to fit more radical models of English governance and an enlivened democratic nation. GOs do, however, need an effective funding base and not continue to rely primarily on elements of DETR regeneration funding. That in itself, can act as a constraint to effective action by government and others at regional level.

The regional administration and regional government agendas fit, especially the former, alongside the government's commitment to its Modernising Government Agenda. Much of this is aimed at affecting the way in which local government and regional quangos work. However, it does need to be considered simultaneously alongside the way in which central government itself works. This is the real challenge of the regionalism agenda—it is more about changing central government—not just about regional institutions. Perhaps the debate has become too embedded in the latter and in its newly created institutions. There needs to be a more sensible balance to the debate itself.

An embryo challenge of regional administrative reform, on a new agenda of coordinated integration of policies across governmental departments has since 1997 led to significant openings which can and sometimes do challenge the fundamental nature of Whitehall decision-making. Allied to the wider debates on devolution and constitutional reform in the UK, the new English GOs, and their associated regional structures are also providing important challenges to the judgements (Stewart 1998) about how the English are to be governed. Certainly if joined-up government is to become a reality then the lessons from the GOs should be crucial learning for a new government of the English for the twenty-first century.

REFERENCES

Association of District Councils. 1995. *Integrated Regional Offices*, London: ADC Economic Development Committee, 5 May.

Association of Metropolitan Authorities. 1995. *Regionalism: The Local Government Dimension*, London: AMA.

Audit Commission. 1989. *Urban Regeneration and Economic Development: The Local Government Dimension*, London, HMSO.

S. Ayres and P. Davis. 2000. *Welcome to the Party? Inclusion, Mutuality and difference in the West Midlands Regional Development Agency network in the United Kingdom*, paper to fourth International Research Symposium on Public Management, Erasmus University, Rotterdam, 10–11 April.

S. Baine, J. Bennington, and J. Russell. 1992. *Changing Europe*, London: Bedford Square Press.

R. Batley and G. Stoker. 1990. (Eds.), *Local Government and Europe*, London: Macmillan.

R. Bennett. 1995. *Meeting Business Needs in Britain: Engaging the Business Community through New Style Chambers*, London: British Chambers of Commerce.

——— , P. Wicks and A. McCoshen. 1994. *Local Experiment and Business Services: Britain's experiment with Training and Enterprise Councils*, London: UCL Press).

G. Bentley and J. Gibney. 2000. (Eds.), *Building a competitive region: Regional Development Agencies and Business Change*, London: Ashgate Press.

R.W. Blac. 2000. *Supporting democratic scrutiny by public audit,* London: Public Management and Policy Association.

J. Bradbury and J. Mawson. 1997. (Eds.*), British Regionalism and Devolution*, London: Jessica Kingsley.

R. Butler. 1993. "The Evolution of the Civil Service," *Public Administration*, Vol. 71, pp. 395–406.

Cabinet Office. 1994. *Continuity and Change,* Cmd.2627, London: HMSO.

——— . 1995. *The Civil Service, Taking forward Continuity and Change*, Cmd 2748, London: HMSO.

——— . 2000. *Reaching Out, the role of central government at regional and local level*, a report of the Performance and Innovation Unit, London.

——— . 2000b. *National Strategy for Neighbourhood Renewal: a framework for consultation,* executive summary.

Campaign for the English Regions. 2000. *Publicity pack,* Newcastle.

S. Chen and T. Wright. 2000. (Eds.), *The English Question*, Fabian Society: London.

Commission of the European Communities, Directorate-General for Regional Policies, *Committee of the Regions*, Factsheet, 11–2–94.

Conservative Party. 1992. *Manifesto 1992: The Best Future for Britain*, London Conservative Party.

Coopers and Lybrand/BITC. 1992. *Growing Business in the UK: Lessons from Continental Europe*, London: Business in the Community.

A. Coulson. 1990. *Devolving Power: The case for Regional Government*, London: Fabian Society.

——— . 1997. "Business Partnerships and Regional Government," *Policy and Politics*, Vol. 25, No. 1, pp. 31–38.

Department of the Environment. 1993a. *News Release 4 November*, London: Department of the Environment.

——— . 1993b. *New Regional Offices*, Fact Sheet No. 1, London: Department of the Environment.

——— . 1993c. *Single Regeneration Budget*, Fact Sheet No. 2, London: Department of the Environment.

——— . 1993d. *Single Regeneration Budget, Note on Principles*, London: Department of the Environment.

J. Dungey and I. Newman. 1999. (Eds.), *The new regional agenda*, London: Local Government Information Unit.

——— . 2000. *The democratic region*, London: Local Government Information Unit.

H. Elcock and M. Keating. 1998. (Eds.*), Remaking the Union: Devolution and British Politics in the 1990s*, London: Frank Cass, 1998.

T. W. Eser. 1996. *Evolution of the Regional Economic and Urban Policy Institutions in the West Midlands*, UK: Institute of Local Government Studies, University of Birmingham.

M. Fell. 1995. *The CBI's Views on the Government Offices in the Regions*, Paper to Association of Metropolitan Authorities Annual Conference, Sheffield, 12 October.

C. Foster and F. Plowden. 1996. *The State under Stress*, Buckingham: Open University Press.

J. Foster. 1995. "MPs attack powers of regional viceroys," *Independent on Sunday,* 5 February.

P. Garside and M. Hebbert. 1989. (Eds.), *British Regionalism 1900–2000*, London: Mansell.

Government Offices for the Regions. 1996. *GO-MINIS 2*, London: Department of Trade and Industry, Department of the Environment, Department for Education and Employment, Department of Transport.

Government Offices Central Unit. 1995. *Government Offices for the Regions, Senior Management Review*, Consultation Report.

C. Gray. 1994. *Government Beyond the Centre*, London: Macmillan.

A. Harding et al. 1996. *Regional Government in Britain: An Economic Solution?* Bristol: Policy Press.

C. Harvie1994. *The Rise of Regional Europe*, London: Routledge, 1994.

M. Hebbert. 1989. "Britain in a Europe of Regions." in P. Garside and M. Hebbert (Eds.), *British Regionalism 1900–2000*, London: Mansell.

P. Hennessy. 1989. *Whitehall*, London: Fontana.

D.M. Hill. 2000. *Urban policy and politics in Britain*, London: Macmillan.

B.W. Hogwood. 1995. *The Integrated Regional Offices and the Single Regeneration Budget*, London: Commission for Local Democracy, Research Report 13.

——. 1996. *Mapping the Regions, Boundaries, Co-ordination and Government*, Bristol, Policy Press.

House of Commons. 1995. *Trade and Industry Committee*, Fourth Report, session 1994–95, London: HMSO.

——. *Treasury and Civil Service Select Committee*, Sixth Report, session 1988–89, London: HMSO.

P. John. 1996. "Centralisation, decentralisation and the European Union: the dynamics of triadic relationships," *Public Administration*, Vol. 74, No. 2, pp. . 293–312.

B. Jones and M. Keating. 1995. (Eds.), *The European Union and the Regions*, Oxford: Clarenden.

N. Lewis. 1992. *Inner City Regeneration: The Demise of Regional and Local Government*, Milton Keynes: Open University Press.

J. Mawson. 1996. "The re-emergence of the regional agenda in the English regions: new patterns of urban and regional governance?" *Local Economy*, Vol. 10, No. 4, pp. 300–325.

——. 1997. "The English Regional Debate: Toward Regional Governance or Government," in J. Bradbury and J. Mawson (Eds.), *British Regionalism and Devolution*, London: Jessica Kingsley.

—— et al. 1994. *The Single Regeneration Budget: the stocktake*, Birmingham: School of Public Policy, University of Birmingham.

J. Mawson and K. Spencer. 1997. "The Origins and operation of the Government Offices for the English Regions," in J. Bradbury and J. Mawson (Eds.), *British Regionalism and Devolution*, London: Jessica Kingsley, pp. 158–179.

——. "Pillars of Strength? The Government Offices for the English Regions." in S. Hardy, M. Hebbert and B. Malbon (Eds.), *Region Building*, (proceedings of the Regional Studies Association Annual Conference.

C. Moore and J. Richardson.1989. *Local Partnership and the Unemployment Crisis in Britain*, London: Unwin Hyman.

National Audit Office. 1990. *Regenerating the Inner Cities*, London: HMSO.

Regional Policy Commission, chaired by B. Millan. 1996. *Renewing the Regions: Strategies for Regional Economic Development*, Report of the Regional Policy Commission, Sheffield: PAVIC Publications.

R.A.W. Rhodes. 1997., *Understanding Governance: Policy networks, governance, reflexivity and accountability*, Buckingham: Open University Press.

D. Ritchie. 1996. *The Role of the Government Offices of the Regions in National Identity and Development—Achievements of the first two years*, Paper to Public Policy Seminar, Queen Mary and Westfield College, University of London, 15 April.

P. Roberts and T. Hart. 1996. *Regional Strategy and Partnership in European Programmes*, York: Joseph Rowntree Foundation.

J. Shutt. 2000. "New Regional Development Agencies in England: wicked issues," in G. Bentley and J. Gibney (Eds.), op.cit.

C. Skelcher. 1998. *The Appointed State: quasi-governmental organisations and democracy*, Buckingham: Open University Press.

K. Spencer. 1988. "Public Policy and Industrial Decline in the West Midlands Region of the United Kingdom," in J.J. Hesse (Ed.), *Regional Structural Change and Industrial Policy in International Perspective*, Baden-Baden: Nomos Verlagsgesellschaft.

—— et al. 1986. *Crisis in the Industrial Heartland*, Oxford: Clarendon.

—— and C. Kunz. 1993. *Building Effective Local Partnerships*, Luton: National Council of Voluntary Organisations and Local Government Management Board.

K. Spencer and J. Mawson. 1997. *Whitehall and the Reorganisation of Regional Offices in England*, ESRC end of project report, ESRC Award L124251024.

—— . 1988a. *Toward Policy Co-ordination at Regional Level*, ESRC Whitehall research programme findings.

—— . 1988b. "Government Offices and Policy Co-ordination in the English Regions," *Local Governance*, Vol. 24, No. 2, pp. 101–109.

—— . 2000. "Transforming regional government offices in England: a new Whitehall agenda," in R.A.W. Rhodes (Ed.), *Transforming British politics, Vol. 2, Changing roles and relationships*, London: Macmillan.

J. Stewart. 1998. "In Support of Judgement," *Local Government Studies*, Vol. 24, No. 3, pp. 67–79

M. Stewart. 1994. "Between Whitehall and Town Hall: The realignment of urban regeneration policy in England," *Policy and Politics*, Vol. 22, No. 2.

G. Stoker, B. Hogwood, and W. Bullman,. 1995. *Regionalism*, Luton: Local Government Management Board.

D. Storey. 1994. *Understanding the Small Business Sector*, London, Routledge.

U. Wannop. 1995. *The Regional Imperative*, London: Jessica Kingsley.

West Midlands Local Government Association. 1998. *Making the West Midlands Work, a Regional Chamber for the West Midlands—a consultation paper* (WMLGA).

S. Young. 1982. "Regional Offices of the Department of the Environment: their roles and influences in the 1970s," in B.W. Hogwood and M. Keating (Eds.), *Regional Government in England*, Oxford: Oxford University Press.

Chapter 4

GLOBALIZATION AND CHANGES IN INDUSTRIAL CONCENTRATION: STATE AND REGIONAL EXPORTS FROM AMERICA'S HEARTLAND, 1988 TO 1997

Lawrence S. Davidson
Global Business Information Network, Kelley School of Business, Bloomington, IN

SUMMARY AND CONCLUSIONS

This paper is a first-step toward understanding how changes in globalization in the 1990s affected the industrial concentration of export sales in America's Heartland (defined in this paper as the following seven states: Kentucky, Illinois, Indiana, Michigan, Ohio, Tennessee, and Wisconsin). Two measures of concentration, based on sector share of export sales, are measured and compared for each of the seven states, the region, and the US. The first of these measures, Top 3, is the sum of the shares of the three largest export industries in 1988 for each state and region. The second measure, Top 12, is defined as the sum of the absolute difference of the actual sector share from 8.33 (the sector share that would prevail if each of the 12 largest export sectors had equal shares of exports and these 12 sectors exhausted all export sales.) This is a measure of concentration (or diversification) because its value would equal zero if all industries had equal shares. The value of Top 12 increases as sector exports are less equally distributed across industries.

This paper examines changes in the structure and concentration of merchandise exports from the Midwestern region to Canada, Mexico, and the rest of the world (ROW). More specifically, we examine the impacts of globalization on the export shares to Canada, Mexico, and ROW from key Midwestern industries. We examine to what extent globalization has caused Midwestern sector export shares to become more or less equal.

Following is a list of facts and conclusions drawn from the analysis.

1. Industry shares changed markedly between 1988 and 1997.
2. As one might expect, the degree of industrial export concentration was negatively related to size of region. In 1988, the US was the least concentrated region, followed by the region, and then, generally, the states. Michigan was, by far, the most concentrated state, largely because of its strong dependence on transportation equipment exports.
3. Export sector concentration between 1988 and 1997 changed relatively little for the US, though its exports to the ROW became more concentrated. That was largely because of the electronic equipment sector's rapid export growth. Concentration in US exports to Canada and Mexico changed little.
4. In contrast, the region's industrial export concentration generally fell, especially to Mexico—and to the smallest extent to ROW.
5. Comparing the US and region experience, it appears that while the US became more concentrated in exports to ROW (perhaps a response to worldwide globalization), the region's exports to North America became more diversified (perhaps a larger response to continental globalization.)
6. Changes in export sector concentration measures varied significantly by export state and export destination. For example, Michigan's exports to Mexico become much less concentrated while Tennessee's became more concentrated. In both cases the main driver was the transportation equipment sector.
7. There were five cases of significantly increased export sector concentration between 1988 and 1997. Ohio, Tennessee, and Kentucky were involved in three of them. Only one of these cases involved Mexico as a destination. Transportation equipment (TE) and industrial machinery and computer equipment (IMCE) were involved in most of these cases.
8. There were 16 cases of significantly decreased export sector concentration between 1988 and 1997. All of the four (or five the seven) largest changes of increased export sector diversification involved Mexico. States showing the largest increases in diversification were Michigan, Kentucky, Wisconsin, Illinois, and Indiana. Diversification increases involved a large number of industries.

9. We can summarize the last two points as follows:
   Increases in concentration: Canada and ROW — US, Ohio, Tennessee, Kentucky
   TE and IMCE
   Decreases in concentration: Mexico — Region, Michigan, Kentucky, Wisconsin, Illinois, and Indiana
   IMCE, TE, FM, CHEM, AGR
10. TE and IMCE were the two largest export sectors in the region in 1988.
11. The region's TE concentration to both Canada and Mexico fell significantly. But various states had differing experiences. Consider three divergent cases:

    Michigan saw TE's share to all three destinations—Mexico, Canada, and ROW—fall.

    Indiana and Tennessee's TE shares rose to all three destinations.

    Kentucky's TE share to Mexico fell but increased dramatically to Canada.
12. The US's and the region's IMCE concentration varied little, though the region's export share of IMCE did fall to all three destinations.

    Wisconsin and Illinois had the region's largest IMCE shares in 1988—and these two states had the largest concentration declines between 1988 and 1997 to all three destinations.

    Kentucky's IMCE share to Mexico increased, despite a share decline to Canada and ROW.
13. Changes in concentration may be related to overall export sales performance. For example, the region's export sales to Mexico increased by 331% and concentration in region exports to Mexico generally decreased between 1988 and 1997. No significant increases in concentration to Mexico were found. In short, with respect to Mexico, fast growth rates translated into increased sector diversification of exports. In contrast, the region's exports to Canada grew by a much slower 109%. Most of the more significant cases of increased concentration involved Canada (or the US.) In the case of Canada, where overall export sales growth was slower, the major export industries, TE and IMCE maintained and increased their shares.
14. State-level evidence both supports and contradicts a simple relationship between export sales and sector concentration changes. Tennessee, Wisconsin, and Michigan had the strongest growth rates to Mexico. These same states each had very large decreases in concentration to Mexico. Ohio had the slowest growth of sales to Mexico and one of the smallest decreases in concentration. Kentucky and Tennessee had the fastest export sales increases to Canada. Notice that Michigan had

the slowest export sales growth to Canada and one of the largest decreases in concentration. Export shares from Michigan to Canada became more equal as TE's share declined.

15. In short, though rapid export sales may coincide with increased export sector diversification, slow export sales may also go along with increased diversification. But does the export sales growth rate cause concentration or vice versa? If the latter, then it would help to know whether, for example an increased diversification was the result of a relatively rapid increase in one or more minor industrial sectors at the expense of a major one; or if the increased diversification resulted from simply a decline in exports of one of the major sectors.
16. Herein may reside the main policy implication of this project. Should changes in export sector diversification be positively and causally related to a region's export sales growth under globalization, then policies like those designed to enhance infrastructure building and clustering might lead to both more balanced export sales among sectors and a higher rate of growth of export sales.

INTRODUCTION

Background

A self-sufficient economic region produces all that it needs. In a world with impenetrable trade barriers, this self-sufficient region neither imports nor exports. Assuming unfettered competition and relatively diversified tastes for goods and services, the region produces a wide variety of goods and services and has a very diversified production base. This wide base implies representation from a large number of industrial sectors that produce relatively equal shares of output (As the number of industries approaches infinity, the relative output share of each industry approaches equality at zero. Of course, the shares of output would approach the composition of the demand for goods and services with less than an infinite number of sectors).

David Ricardo's concept of comparative advantage applied to a world without significant trade barriers forcefully argues against self-sufficiency. If each economic region specializes in that which it has a comparative advantage and trades with other regions, then each region benefits through specialization. In this case, a region with relatively diversified tastes for goods and services might be home to a small number of industries with large relative export shares. Since comparative advantage is rarely taken to extreme, the region might have representation from a large number of industries, but only a few would have large shares of output. In this region, depending on the structure of imports and exports, the export shares among the industries could differ markedly.

Consider next an open region that is confronted with a reduction in the cost of two-way trade (perhaps caused by a new trade regulation or a reduction in transportation or communications costs.) This allows the region to take fuller advantage of the benefits of comparative advantage and leads to increases in both imports and exports. With respect to exports, one would not expect equal responses from all industrial sectors for several reasons:

- The export response might be more than proportional to each industry's historical global comparative advantage (or competitiveness)
- Changes in industrial composition and technology may alter historical global comparative advantage
- The elasticity of supply might differ significantly across sectors because of input constraints
- Differences in the stage of development (or other factors affecting the composition of the demand for goods and services) of new foreigner buyers may increase worldwide demand for some goods and services relative to others.

In short, there would be two conflicting impacts on this region's industrial composition of exports. First, historical comparative advantage suggests that the shares of export-intensive industries would increase at the expense of others. This would make export shares more unequal and weighted toward those with the largest previous shares. Second, to the extent that the reduction in the cost of trade is accompanied by supply constraints and changes in demand and comparative advantage, the relative shares of industries with previously large shares might decrease. This second factor could:

- Increase export share inequality if the new (few) export leaders are more effective than the past ones—that is, their export shares become larger than their predecessors.
- Decrease export share inequality if new export leaders increase their shares at the expense of their predecessors—that is, the shares of previous low-share sectors increase at the expense of previous high-share sectors (but not by so much as to basically change share places.)
- Decrease export share inequality due to vertical industrial clustering. Vertical clustering yields expected productivity and innovation gains via face-to-face communications and interactions. For example, an original equipment manufacturer might expect to increase productivity through closer proximity to machine tool producers. (Note: clustering could increase share inequality

if it brings more suppliers to a locality who are vertically linked and are all considered part of the same broad industry classification.)

It is this kind of process that the World Bank refers to in "Creating Cities that Work" (*World Bank Policy and Research Bulletin*). Consider the opening statement of the article, "As the twenty-first century begins, industrial and developing countries alike face the same challenge: how to reap the benefits of globalization." The main point is that globalization is driving change and those countries and subnational entities that do not compete globally are likely to fall (further) behind. The World Bank suggests that subnational governments can improve their environments in many ways, including improving infrastructure, efficiently providing services, creating and enforcing legal rights, attracting human and non-human capital, and designing policies that create a critical mass of specific industries. By creating a better climate for exporting companies, these changes—in the face of growing global opportunities—may evoke a larger proportional export response from sectors with heretofore smaller export shares.

Cities in the US are impacted as much by changes in North America as by worldwide phenomena. While the North American Free Trade Agreement (NAFTA) did not take affect until 1995, the preceding Canada-US Free Trade Agreement, and increasing trade flows between the US and Mexico created more economic integration in North America. Inasmuch, we evaluate changes in industrial export shares of America's Heartland to Canada, Mexico, NAFTA (Canada plus Mexico), and the rest of the world (ROW).

The Region

Throughout this paper "region" refers to the seven states that comprise the east north- central region of the US (Illinois, Indiana, Michigan, Ohio, and Wisconsin) plus Kentucky and Tennessee. We investigate changes between 1988 and 1997 in export sales of the 12 largest export sectors from this region. According to Geoffrey Hewings, Graham R. Schindler, and Philip R. Israilevich (Chicago Fed Letter) the east north-central region forms a regional economy. They find that globalization-induced clustering has occurred at the region, rather than at the state level. If this is true, then the export distribution of the region might have become more diversified while any particular state became more specialized.

Industrial Export Sectors

Twelve sectors were chosen because they had the largest export sales to Canada and Mexico during the period. All industries in the seven states sold \$921 billion exports to the world between 1988 and 1997. Of that amount, \$461 billion—approximately 50 percent—went to Canada and Mexico. The 12 sectors were responsible for $424 billion (or 92%) of that amount.

The largest sector in the region exporting to Canada and Mexico was the transportation equipment (TE) Sector. It contributed 45 percent of the total exports of the region to NAFTA. The Table 1 shows the relative contributions to the $424 billion from the 12 sectors in the region during the 1988 to 1997 time period:

The Table 2 shows the growth of exports to the NAFTA countries from the region by these sectors from 1988 to 1997. Export change ranged from a low of 23 percent for fabricated metals products (FM) to a high of 832 percent for furniture (FURN). Notice that all but two of the sectors grew faster than TE—

Table 1: Region Exports to Canada and Mexico, 1988 to 1997

	(billions of dollars)
Transportation equipment (TE)	191
Industrial machinery and computer equipment (IMCE)	81
Electronic and electrical equipment (EE)	34
Fabricated metal products (FM)	25
Chemicals and allied products (CHEM)	24
Primary metals industries (PM)	17
Rubber and plastics products (R&P)	13
Sophisticated instruments (SOPH)	10
Food products (FOOD)	9
Paper products (PP)	7
Furniture (FURN)	7
Printing and publishing (P&P)	6
Total—12 industries	424
All industries	464

Table 2: Percent Change, by Sector Sectors (Dollar value of exports sequence) Export Sales, 1988 to 1997

Transportation equipment (TE)	88
Industrial machinery and computer equipment (IMCE)	180
Electronic and electrical equipment (EE)	229
Fabricated metal products (FM)	23
Chemicals and allied products (CHEM)	239
Primary metals Industries (PM)	106
Rubber and plastics products (R&P)	270
Sophisticated instruments (SOPH)	319
Food products (FOOD)	320
Paper products (PP)	379
Printing and publishing (P&P)	95

therefore closing the export share gap somewhat over this time period. The average growth rate for all the region sectors to Canada and Mexico was 127 percent.

Region Export Performance 1988 to 1997

Next we examine the region's exports by state—the sum from 1988 to 1997 (Table 3). This seven-state region shipped $920 billion of exports to the world—representing almost 20 percent of the US total exports to the world. It accounted for over 32 percent of the nation's exports to NAFTA (41 percent of US exports to Canada and 13 percent of the nation's sales to Mexico). Michigan is the largest exporting state in the region. It accounted for 28 percent of the region's exports to the world and 41 percent of the region's exports to NAFTA. Despite its northern location, Michigan accounted for 43 percent of the region's exports to Mexico.

US export sales to the world increased by 120 percent between 1988 and 1997. They grew by 146 percent and 246 percent, respectively to Canada and Mexico. The region's exports grew more slowly than the nation's to Canada (109 percent) but more rapidly to Mexico (331 percent). Putting these facts together, the region's share of exports to NAFTA did not change much since the rate of change of exports to NAFTA was approximately equal to the rate of change to the world (Table 4).

We can classify the states according to whether or not the share of exports going to NAFTA increased or decreased.

Michigan was the only state with a decreasing share of exports to NAFTA—largely because of smaller share to Canada. Michigan's exports grew at the slowest pace of any of the seven states. Of course, Michigan still had the highest dependence of all these states on NAFTA (73 percent of Michigan's world exports).

Table 3: Total, 1988 to 1997 Exports to (billions of dollars):

Exports from:	*Canada*	*Mexico*	*NAFTA*	*World*	*NAFTA/ World*
US	1,005.0	414.8	1420.0	4,793.2	.30
Region	407.4	53.4	460.7	920.6	.50
Michigan	163.9	22.9	186.8	255.4	.73
Ohio	85.0	6.8	91.8	193.7	.47
Illinois	59.9	11.2	71.2	197.0	.36
Indiana	36.9	3.3	40.1	83.9	.48
Wisconsin	25.0	2.8	27.8	77.4	.36
Tennessee	20.1	4.6	24.7	64.1	.39
Kentucky	16.5	1.8	18.3	49.2	.37

Table 4: Percentage Change in Exports from 1988 to 1997 to:

Exports from:	*Canada*	*Mexico*	*NAFTA*	*World World*	*NAFTA/*
US	146	246	172	120	1.4
Region	109	331	128	123	1.0
Michigan	28	367	56	65	0.9
Ohio	159	184	160	122	1.3
Illinois	205	280	215	153	1.4
Indiana	244	272	246	176	1.4
Wisconsin	163	497	181	137	1.3
Tennessee	315	568	352	241	1.5
Kentucky	332	264	325	196	1.7

Kentucky and Tennessee, the two smallest exporting states, had the highest growth rates of exports to the world and to NAFTA. These states had the largest changes in NAFTA share as evidenced by the ratio of their export growth to NAFTA relative to (divided by) their export growth to the world. The states, in order of increased NAFTA share were: Kentucky, Tennessee, Illinois, Indiana, Wisconsin, Ohio, and Michigan (share decreased). It is notable that Indiana had a relatively large share of exports to NAFTA *and* a relatively large increase in share. Whereas Kentucky, Ohio, Indiana, and Illinois had relatively equal growth rates to Canada, and Mexico, Michigan, Wisconsin, and Tennessee tended to favor Mexico.

CHANGES IN INDUSTRIAL EXPORT CONCENTRATION, 1988 TO 1997

Top 3 Industries, 1988

IMCE and TE were among the top three industries for both the US and the region (See Appendix 1, Table 1).

The third sector among the top three depended upon who was sending to whom:

Exporter	**Destination**	**Third Sector**
US or region	ROW	CHEM
US or region	Mexico	EE
US	Canada	EE
Region	Canada	FM

Export Concentration, 1988, US and the Region

Generally, US exports were more diversified than the region's in 1988 using both measures—Top 3 and Top 12. Top 3 measures the share of the Top 3 industries for each exporter area-destination combination. The table below shows, for example, that the Top 3 share of US exports to Canada was 61 in 1988. The region Top 3 share to Canada was 72. Therefore, the US was less concentrated (more diversified) than the region to Canada. The table confirms that result for the other two destinations as well—Mexico and ROW.

Top 12 is defined as the sum of the absolute differences of the shares of each of the Top 12 industries from 8.33 (8.33 is the share that each of the 12 industries would have had if the Top 12 industries equally shared all exports). Top 12 would have had a value of zero if exports were equally shared by the Top 12 industries. Top 12 increases whenever sector shares do not equal 8.33—so it is a measure of inequality of share. Notice that the Top 12 measure confirms the conclusion that the US is generally less concentrated than the region (region is relatively less diversified) to all three destinations. Quantitatively, Top 12 tends to show larger differences than Top 3. For example, the Top 3 measure shows that the US is 47% less concentrated than the region in its exports to Mexico. The Top 12 measure indicates a 59% percentage difference in concentration.

Both the US and the region were very heavily concentrated in exports to Canada in 1988. In contrast, the region's concentration was sharply higher than the US's with respect to exports to Mexico.

Top 3/Top 12 Values in 1988

Destination	*Exporter/US*	*Region*	*Percentage Difference*
ROW	45/57	62/81	38/42
Canada	61/82	72/104	18/27
Mexico	47/59	69/94	47/59

Export Concentration, 1988, Seven States

Table 5 below groups export states and region by concentration intensity according to their Top 12 value:

Very High	greater than 105
High	91–104
Medium	74–90
Low	less than 74

There were large discrepancies across the export regions in terms of industrial concentration in 1988. At two extremes were Michigan and Tennessee with

Table 5: Destination (Canada, Mexico, or Rest of World)

Export State	*Concentration Category*			
	Very High	*High*	*Medium*	*Low*
Michigan	Can, Mex, ROW			
Indiana		Mex, Can	ROW	
Region		Mex, Can	ROW	
Kentucky		Mex, Can	ROW	
Wisconsin		Can	Mexico, ROW	
Ohio			Can, Mex, ROW	
Illinois			Can, Mex, ROW	
Tennessee			Can, ROW	Mex
US			Can, Mex	ROW

respect to exports to Mexico. Whereas Michigan's Top 3 export sectors sold 89% of the state's exports to Mexico, Tennessee's Top 3 were responsible for a 39% share.

Michigan holds the distinction of being the most concentrated area in 1988 to all three export areas—ROW, Canada, and Mexico. Between 75% and 89% of Michigan's exports were from its Top 3 industries in 1988. Michigan's high concentration was largely the result of a very large share of exports from the TE industry—TE accounted for 72% and 70% of Michigan's exports to Canada and Mexico, respectively.

Indiana (TE and IMCE), the region (TE and IMCE), and Kentucky (TE, IMCE, and CHEM) had high sector concentrations for their export sales to Canada and Mexico.

Wisconsin's (IMCE and TE) sectors had high concentration only to Canada.

Ohio, Illinois, and Tennessee were the states with the least industrial concentration of exports sales. Tennessee had the least concentration—most diversification—in its exports to Mexico. The Top 12 score was only 38—and the share of its largest three export sectors to Mexico was only 39%.

The most diversified export region/destination couple was the US to ROW.

Changes in Export Concentration, 1988 to 1997

We examined nine export areas and three export destinations—giving 27 area/destination export share change combinations. Appendix 2 contains all share change information.

There was a much greater tendency for an export area to experience a decline in export destination concentration as evidenced either by a reduction in the share of its Top 3 industries or a more equal distribution of export share among its Top 12 industries (Table 6).

Table 6: Changes in Industry Export Concentration, 1988 to 1997

Export State/Region	*Destination (Canada, Mexico, or Rest of World) Concentration Change Category*		
	*Large Change**	*Medium Change**	*Small Change**
Michigan	Mex TE, FM, R&P	Can TE, FM	ROW IMCE
Indiana	Mex IMCE, CHEM	**Can** **TE, IMCE**	ROW CHEM, EE
Region	Mex TE, IMCE	Can TE	ROW IMCE, EE
Kentucky	Mex TE, CHEM, IMCE	**ROW** **TE**	**Can** **TE, IMCE**
Wisconsin	Mex IMCE, AGR	Can IMCE, TE	ROW AGR
Ohio	**Can** **TE, IMCE**	Mex PM	ROW TE, IMCE
Illinois	Mex IMCE	Can IMCE	ROW IMCE
Tennessee	**Mex** **IMCE**	Can EE	ROW CHEM
US	**ROW** **EE**	Can TE	Mex TE, EE

*Items in **boldface** were positive changes (increases) in Top 3/Top 12. These indicate increased concentration. Large increases were 10 or above; medium changes were from 5 to 9; small changes were 1to 4.

Items not in boldface were negative changes (decreases) in Top 3/Top 12. These indicate decreases in concentration. Large changes were –19 or higher; medium changes were from –5 to –18; small changes were from –1 to –4.

Increased Export Concentration

All references to point totals can be found in Appendix 2. Both the Top 12 and Top 3 changes are indicated below.

Notice that all but one of the notable increases in concentration did *not* involve Mexico:

- Ohio to Canada increased by 15/13 points. (TE and IMCE)
- Kentucky to ROW increased by 12/10 points. (TE)
- US to ROW increased by 11/1 points (EE)
- Kentucky to Canada increased by 5/1 point (TE and IMCE)

Kentucky was the only area to have increased concentrations to two destinations, ROW and Canada.

Tennessee had conflicting results for Top 3 and Top 12. Concentration rose for Top 12 because TE increased by 20 points. However, since TE was not a Top 3 industry for Tennessee, Top 3 declined overall, especially because of share decreases in CHEM and EE.

Decreased Export Concentration

Michigan and Wisconsin were the only two states or regions to show significant decreases in concentration to all three export destinations.

Most export areas experienced some degree of decreasing concentration. Twenty-one of the 27 combinations had decreases in concentration. Of the 21, 16 had changes that were 5 percentage points or more.

The four largest decreases in concentration involved exports to Mexico:

- Michigan to Mexico decreased by 34/14 points (TE, FM, R&P)
- Kentucky to Mexico decreased by 21/26 points (TE, CHEM, IMCE)
- Wisconsin to Mexico decreased by 19/20 points (IMCE, AGR)
- Illinois to Mexico decreased by 28/15 points (IMCE)

Twelve medium decreases in concentration were:

- Indiana to Mexico decreased by 14/22 (IMCE, CHEM)
- Wisconsin to Canada decreased by 14/13 (IMCE, TE)
- Region to Mexico decreased by 14/7 (IMCE, TE)
- Michigan to Canada decreased by 14/12 (TE, FM, TE)
- Tennessee to Canada decreased by 13/9 (EE)
- Wisconsin to ROW decreased by 10/8 (AGR)
- Tennessee to Row decreased by 9/3 (CHEM)
- Region to Canada decreased by 8/8 (TE)
- Ohio to Mexico decreased by 7/12 (PM)
- US to Canada decreased by 7/5 (TE)

- Michigan to ROW decreased by 6/3 (IMCE)
- Illinois to Canada decreased by 5/8 (IMCE)

Industry Analysis

Transportation Equipment

TE was one of the Top 3 industry sectors for the US and region in1988. Table 2 in Appendix 1 summarizes changes in the share of TE in each of the 9 export areas.

Relative importance of TE to Canada

- Declining in those areas that had the highest reliance in 1988 æ Michigan, the region, US
- Rising in Indiana, Kentucky, Ohio, and Tennessee

Relative importance of TE to Mexico

- Declining in those areas that had the highest reliance in 1988 æ Michigan, the region, and Kentucky
- Rising in Indiana and Tennessee

Relative importance of TE to ROW

- Declining in those areas that had the highest reliance in 1988 æ Michigan and Ohio
- Rising in Kentucky, Indiana, and Tennessee

Michigan was, by far, the most TE concentrated export area.

Yet, the share of TE in Michigan's total exports fell to all three export destinations. Whereas it fell marginally to the ROW, the decline was much larger for Mexico and Canada. Thus, Michigan is coming to depend relatively less on TE for exports.

The region, like Michigan, was very heavily dependent on TE exports. Its dependence on Mexico and Canada fell.

TE's concentration in Indiana and Tennessee increased to all three export destinations—thus TE is becoming much more important to the export missions of those two states.

Kentucky's TE export shares declined to Mexico, but increased dramatically to ROW and Canada.

For Ohio and Illinois, TE generally increased its share to Canada

US's TE decreased its share to Canada.

Industrial Machinery

Table 3 in Appendix 1 summarizes changes in the share of IMCE in each of the nine export areas.

Relative importance of IMCE to Canada

- Declining in those areas that had the highest concentrations in 1988—Illinois, Wisconsin, Kentucky, and Indiana
- Small increases in the region, Ohio, and Michigan

Relative Importance of IMCE in Mexico

- Declining in those areas that has the highest concentrations in 1988—Wisconsin, Illinois, and Indiana
- Moderate declines in the region, US, and Michigan.
- A large increase in Kentucky

Relative Importance of IMCE in ROW

- Very small decline in the largest export state—Wisconsin
- Very large decline in second largest export state—Illinois.
- Small increases in Indiana and US

Wisconsin and Illinois were the most important IMCE areas for all three destinations—ROW, Canada, and Mexico. The IMCE share in both Wisconsin and Illinois fell to these destinations. Only in the case of Wisconsin exports to ROW was the decrease small.

The IMCE share of an area's exports did not increase very much, except in the case of IMCE's share of Kentucky's exports to Mexico. Kentucky's IMCE export share to Canada and ROW declined.

IMCE export shares to Mexico from Ohio and Michigan rose by small amounts—and showed little change to Canada and ROW.

REFERENCES

Geoffrey Hewings, Graham R. Schindler, and Philip R. Israilevich, "Interstate Trade Among Midwest Economies," Chicago Fed Letter, May 1998.

Michael E. Porter, "Clusters and Competition: New Agenda for Companies, Governments, and Institutions, " Harvard Business School, *Division of Research Working Paper*, 98-080, September 1997.

David Ricardo, *On the Principles of Political Economy and Taxation*, originally published in London in 1817, since reprinted by a number of publishers.

World Bank, "Creating Cities that Work in the New Global Economy," *World Bank Policy and Research Bulletin* (October-December 1998), pp. 1-4.

APPENDIX 1

Table 1. Exports 1988 Share of Exports (by percentages)

USA					
ROW		*Canada*		*Mexico*	
OTHER	29	OTHER	28	OTHER	35
IMCE	20	TE	25	EE	22
EE	16	IMCE	18	IMCE	15
TE	15	EE	13	TE	11
CHEM	11	CHEM	8	CHEM	9
SOPH	7	FM	4	FM	4
FM	2	SOPH	4	SOPH	4
Regional					
IMCE	22	TE	42	TE	40
OTHER	20	OTHER	19	IMCE	21
TE	20	IMCE	19	OTHER	18
CHEM	16	EE	7	CHEM	8
EE	13	CHEM	6	EE	8
FM	6	FM	4	FM	3
SOPH	3	SOPH	3	SOPH	2

Table 2. TE Exports to Canada, Mexico, and ROW, 1988 and 1997, Percent of total — Absolute deviations from 8.33

	Canada	
	1988	*1997*
MI	63.91688	48.45895
Region	41.49165	33.12635
IN	26.19744	35.69575
USA	26.11089	16.57439
KY	23.67548	38.38094
OH	23.01239	35.44632
TN	14.92098	21.19003
WI	13.42444	9.94312
IL	3.573635	8.697667
	Mexico	
	1988	*1997*
MI	61.21469	44.18248
REGION	32.05532	26.40347
KY	20.09463	2.465726
IN	3.451873	15.09845
WI	2.737847	2.70415
IL	2.328574	0.8178
USA	2.251316	3.835139
TN	0.737341	18.83875
OH	0.164894	2.579155
	ROW	
	1988	*1997*
MI	33.34534	31.93264
OH	21.84942	16.64789
Region	10.2706	11.19326
KY	6.464523	23.38233
USA	5.590047	6.347546
WI	4.555758	1.302029
IN	3.352347	7.963731
TN	0.991591	6.772755
IL	0.711077	0.434199

Table 3. IMCE Exports to Canada, Mexico, and ROW, 1988 and 1997, Percent of total — Absolute deviations from 8.33

	Canada 1988	1997
IL	38.81068	21.94273
WI	31.17507	22.07517
KY	13.00978	6.95139
IN	11.75056	5.904797
USA	8.898928	9.419561
TN	8.123666	5.003976
Region	6.259595	10.52022
OH	3.531406	8.245022
MI	3.048889	7.222709

	Mexico 1988	1997
WI	32.15781	21.70274
IL	27.94548	14.2836
IN	27.61661	19.65343
OH	14.18331	14.15453
REGION	12.8867	9.064155
KY	10.31129	20.50677
USA	6.801772	5.548528
MI	5.799237	5.057135
TN	1.665963	2.948736

	ROW 1988	1997
WI	30.99787	29.68435
IL	29.96103	12.34087
Region	18.74797	13.26747
OH	16.50728	16.319
KY	15.81639	10.57687
USA	10.34239	11.84808
MI	9.366886	7.149516
IN	6.438135	9.93873
TN	4.474072	5.556199

APPENDIX 2

Export Share Changes, Rest of the World, State and Regional Shares in 1988, 1997, and Change

State and Regional Shares in 1988, 1997, and Change

	Top 12	Top 3	IMCE	TE	CHEM	EE	SOPH	FOOD	FM	R&P	PM	AGR	PP	SCGP
WI	88	65	**39.3**	3.8	2.8	5.9	**10.1**	8.8	2.7	0.9	0.4	**15.5**	2.0	0.5
WI	78	57	**38.0**	9.6	4.1	8.1	**13.1**	5.4	3.7	1.3	0.6	**5.8**	2.6	0.7
Change	-10	-8	**-1.3**	5.9	1.3	2.2	**3.0**	-3.4	1.0	0.4	0.3	**-9.7**	0.5	0.3
TN	77	56	**12.8**	**7.3**	**36.1**	4.5	7.1	3.1	2.8	1.6	3.9	4.9	2.9	0.7
TN	68	53	**13.9**	**15.1**	**24.0**	6.7	7.7	5.7	1.9	2.0	2.6	2.8	5.0	0.9
Change	-9	-3	**1.1**	**7.8**	**-12.1**	2.3	0.6	2.5	-0.9	0.3	-1.3	-2.1	2.1	0.2
OH	88	66	**24.8**	**30.2**	**11.4**	5.5	5.5	1.2	4.2	3.1	3.6	1.5	0.7	3.3
OH	84	65	**24.6**	**25.0**	**14.9**	8.2	5.2	0.8	3.2	4.4	3.7	1.8	1.0	2.7
Change	-4	-2	**-0.2**	**-5.2**	**3.5**	2.6	-0.3	-0.4	-1.0	1.4	0.1	0.3	0.3	-0.6
MI	107	75	**17.7**	**41.7**	**15.7**	3.6	3.3	1.8	2.3	1.1	2.1	1.3	1.1	1.1
MI	102	72	**15.5**	**40.3**	**16.5**	5.3	3.6	1.6	3.0	1.3	2.6	0.6	0.8	1.8
Change	-6	-3	**-2.2**	**-1.4**	**0.8**	1.7	0.2	-0.2	0.7	0.2	0.4	-0.8	-0.4	0.7
KY	81	53	**24.1**	**14.8**	**14.3**	3.9	2.5	4.2	1.1	1.5	1.8	5.1	0.5	1.9
KY	93	63	**18.9**	**31.7**	**12.8**	4.7	2.3	4.2	1.7	2.0	1.6	0.6	0.7	2.5
Change	12	10	**-5.2**	**16.9**	**-1.5**	0.8	-0.3	0.1	0.7	0.5	-0.2	-4.5	0.2	0.6
IL	87	65	**38.3**	7.6	**14.1**	**12.3**	5.3	6.2	3.4	2.4	1.7	0.5	0.5	0.4
IL	83	63	**20.7**	7.9	**13.6**	**29.0**	6.1	4.7	3.1	2.5	1.6	1.8	1.9	1.0
Change	-4	-1	**-17.6**	0.3	**-0.5**	**16.7**	0.8	-1.4	-0.3	0.1	-0.2	1.3	1.4	0.6
IN	81	60	**14.8**	11.7	**32.8**	**12.0**	5.4	2.7	1.5	3.3	8.3	1.2	0.8	0.5
IN	80	53	**18.3**	16.3	**26.9**	**7.6**	8.2	2.8	2.9	3.0	5.3	0.8	0.6	0.6
Change	-1	-7	**3.5**	4.6	**-5.9**	**-4.5**	2.8	0.1	1.4	-0.3	-3.0	-0.4	-0.2	0.1
USA	57	45	**18.7**	**13.9**	**12.1**	9.5	6.2	6.1	1.6	1.3	3.9	8.8	2.4	0.6
USA	69	45	**20.2**	**14.7**	**10.6**	16.0	6.9	4.8	2.2	1.5	3.0	4.9	2.1	0.8
Change	11	1	**1.5**	**0.8**	**-1.5**	6.5	0.7	-1.3	0.6	0.2	-0.9	-3.8	-0.4	0.2
Region	81	61	**27.1**	**18.6**	**15.8**	7.5	5.5	3.9	3.0	2.2	2.8	3.2	1.0	1.3
Region	80	57	**21.6**	**19.5**	**15.5**	13.1	6.4	3.4	2.9	2.6	2.5	2.0	1.7	1.5
Change	-1	-5	**-5.5**	**0.9**	**-0.3**	5.6	0.9	-0.5	0.0	0.4	-0.3	-1.2	0.7	0.2

To Canada: State and Regional Shares in 1988, 1997, and Change

	Top 12	Top 3	TE	IMCE	EE	CHEM	FM	PM	R&P	SOPH	FOOD	FURN	PP	SCGP	P&P
WI	102	68	**21.8**	**39.5**	**6.4**	1.9	4.3	1.3	1.8	2.2	1.7	0.6	4.4	0.5	1.3
WI	75	54	**18.3**	**30.4**	**5.7**	4.8	4.5	1.3	3.6	4.8	4.4	0.8	7.1	0.6	2.9
Change	-27	-13	**-3.5**	**-9.1**	**-0.8**	2.9	0.2	0.0	1.8	2.6	2.8	0.2	2.7	0.1	1.6
Tennes:	84	63	**23.3**	**16.5**	**23.2**	9.5	3.1	2.3	5.8	2.4	2.1	1.0	0.6	1.3	3.8
Tennes:	68	54	**29.5**	**13.3**	**10.7**	8.3	3.6	1.7	5.8	3.2	2.8	3.7	3.3	2.7	2.7
Change	-16	-9	**6.3**	**-3.1**	**-12.5**	-1.1	0.5	-0.6	0.0	0.8	0.7	2.7	2.7	1.3	-1.1
Ohio	74	51	**31.3**	**11.9**	4.9	4.6	7.9	**8.3**	4.1	3.3	1.3	0.2	0.7	2.1	0.6
Ohio	97	65	**43.8**	**16.6**	6.3	6.0	4.7	**4.3**	3.1	2.1	1.2	0.8	1.1	2.1	0.5
Change	23	13	**12.4**	**4.7**	1.4	1.4	-3.2	**-3.9**	-1.0	-1.2	0.0	0.7	0.4	0.0	-0.1
Michiga	135	87	**72.2**	**5.3**	2.9	1.9	**9.6**	1.1	0.6	0.5	0.2	0.4	0.5	2.1	0.1
Michiga	118	76	**56.8**	**15.6**	3.5	4.0	**3.2**	2.7	1.4	1.8	0.8	2.7	0.6	1.5	0.3
Change	-17	-12	**-15.5**	**10.3**	0.6	2.1	**-6.4**	1.6	0.8	1.3	0.6	2.3	0.1	-0.6	0.2
Kentuck	91	67	**32.0**	**21.3**	3.0	**13.4**	2.0	7.3	2.0	0.6	3.5	0.2	1.2	2.5	5.9
Kentuck	97	68	**46.7**	**15.3**	6.1	**6.0**	2.3	5.6	2.9	0.9	1.1	1.9	1.7	0.9	3.6
Change	6	1	**14.7**	**-6.1**	3.1	**-7.4**	0.4	-1.7	0.9	0.3	-2.4	1.6	0.5	-1.6	-2.4
Illinois	82	61	4.8	**47.1**	**7.9**	**6.0**	6.0	6.5	3.4	2.1	2.5	0.3	0.5	0.8	8.4
Illinois	80	53	17.0	**30.3**	**14.1**	**8.6**	3.5	4.0	3.4	3.1	3.8	0.7	1.8	0.8	3.0
Change	-2	-8	12.3	**-16.9**	**6.2**	**2.6**	-2.5	-2.5	0.0	1.0	1.3	0.4	1.3	0.0	-5.4
Indiana	93	68	**34.5**	**20.1**	**13.1**	5.4	5.3	10.3	2.5	1.6	1.5	0.2	0.4	1.1	1.2
Indiana	94	69	**44.0**	**14.2**	**11.1**	4.4	3.9	5.1	3.5	4.7	1.3	0.9	0.7	1.4	1.1
Change	1	2	**9.5**	**-5.8**	**-2.1**	-1.0	-1.4	-5.2	1.0	3.1	-0.2	0.7	0.3	0.3	-0.1
USA	82	60	**34.4**	**17.2**	**8.8**	7.0	5.4	4.1	2.3	3.6	2.7	0.3	1.6	1.5	1.5
USA	74	56	**24.9**	**17.7**	**12.9**	8.4	3.7	4.4	2.9	3.9	3.3	1.2	2.1	1.2	1.5
Change	-8	-5	**-9.5**	**0.5**	**4.1**	1.4	-1.7	0.3	0.6	0.3	0.6	0.9	0.5	-0.3	0.0
Region	104	72	**49.8**	**14.6**	5.2	3.6	**7.9**	3.8	1.9	1.4	0.9	0.4	0.7	1.8	1.5
Region	95	64	**41.5**	**18.9**	7.4	5.7	**3.7**	3.5	2.8	2.6	1.8	1.7	1.5	1.5	1.4
Change	-9	-8	**-8.4**	**4.3**	2.1	2.1	**-4.2**	-0.2	0.9	1.2	0.8	1.3	0.8	-0.3	-0.1

To Mexico: State and Regional Shares in 1988, 1997, and Change

	Top 12	Top 3	IMCE	TE	EE	PM	CHEM	PP	R&P	FM	SOPH	FOOD	AGR	SCGP
WI	83	61	40	6	5	2	3	4	5	4	14	3	7	0
WI	64	41	30	6	15	1	8	8	3	5	9	7	2	0
Change	-19	-20	-10	0	10	-1	5	4	-2	1	-5	3	-5	0
TN	38	39	10	9	12	9	17	9	7	5	6	8	2	1
TN	58	29	11	27	9	6	8	5	9	2	2	2	6	1
Change	20	-10	1	18	-2	-2	-9	-4	2	-3	-4	-6	4	0
Ohio	75	60	23	8	7	17	21	1	9	3	3	1	0	3
Ohio	68	48	22	11	12	6	20	3	8	6	1	3	0	3
Change	-7	-12	0	3	4	-11	-1	2	-1	2	-2	1	0	0
Michiga	135	89	14	70	5	2	2	1	2	3	1	0	0	0
Michiga	101	75	13	53	9	2	3	1	6	7	3	0	0	1
Change	-34	-14	-1	-17	4	0	1	0	4	4	3	0	0	1
Kentuck	102	69	19	28	12	2	22	0	2	1	0	2	0	5
Kentuck	81	43	29	6	11	21	9	1	5	3	1	2	1	2
Change	-21	-26	10	-23	0	19	-14	1	3	2	1	0	0	-3
Illinois	84	60	36	11	13	10	6	1	2	2	3	4	0	1
Illinois	55	46	23	8	15	5	11	4	6	5	4	8	4	2
Change	-28	-15	-14	-3	2	-5	5	3	4	3	1	3	4	0
Indiana	96	68	36	12	8	16	16	0	2	1	4	1	0	1
Indiana	82	46	28	23	11	10	8	5	4	3	2	2	0	1
Change	-14	-22	-8	12	3	-6	-8	4	3	2	-2	0	0	0
USA	59	47	15	11	22	4	9	4	4	4	4	5	5	1
USA	63	50	14	12	24	5	8	3	5	4	4	3	4	1
Change	4	2	-1	2	2	0	-1	-1	1	1	0	-1	-2	0
Region	94	69	21	40	8	7	8	1	3	3	2	2	0	1
Region	80	63	17	35	11	4	7	2	6	6	3	2	1	1
Change	-14	-7	-4	-6	3	-3	-1	1	3	3	1	0	1	0

Top 3 Industries Impacting Changes in Concentration from 1988 to 1997

		TE			IMCE			CHEM			EE		
	ROW	CAN	MEX	ROW	CAN	MEX	ROW	CAN	MEX	ROW	CAN	MEX	ROW
Region		-8	-6	-6	4	-4				6			
USA		-10								7	4		
Indiana	5	10	12	4	-6	-8	-6			-5			
Illinois		12		-18	-17	-14				17	6		
Kentucky	17	15	-23	-5	-6	10		-7	-14				
Michigan		-16	-17		10							4	
Ohio	-5	12			5		4					4	
Tennessee	8	6	18				-12		-9		-13		
Wisconsin	6	-4			-9	-10			5			10	
Total	31	17	-16	-25	-19	-26	-14	-7	-18	25	-3	18	0

	PM			AGR			FM			SOPH		Total
	CAN	MEX	ROW	CAN	MEX	ROW	CAN	MEX	ROW	CAN	MEX	
Region							4					-14
USA												1
Indiana	-5	-6										1
Illinois		-5										-14
Kentucky		19										-30
Michigan							-6					-19
Ohio	-4	-11										25
Tennessee											-4	-10
Wisconsin				-10							-5	-8
Total	-9	-3	0	-10	0	0	-2	0			-9	-68

Chapter 5:

GLOBALIZATION AND THE LOCAL UNIVERSITY

John W. Ryan

Chancellor Emeritus, State University of New York, and President Emeritus, Indiana University

There is widespread awareness that "globalization" is "real"; i.e., is a factor that affects the mission and context of the major institutions of current world society—nations that are mature, developing, and under-developed.

"Globalization," then, gives rise to significant environmental (curricular, managerial, research) influences on universities, and such impact can be expected to increase in strength and scope. It should be anticipated that the consequences can be both salubrious and unfortunate, and that they will likely impact the internal character of the university as a universal institution as well as the external relationships of universities within their socio/political contexts.

It is important to consider "globalization" in its broadest context. Too often both protagonists and antagonists limit their review and evaluation too narrowly. Indeed, some commentators limit "globalization" to matters of international trade and investment, others use similarly narrow parameters.

"Globalization," as I shall be using the term, is the web of contacts, impacts, and connections now engulfing the basic institutions of the world in virtually every dimension of activity; demographic, economic, technological, environmental, and political.

Globalization is not coming; it is here. Because it is here, and is so pervasive in its effect on all institutions of society, it must be considered an inescapable issue for the university.

Until now, we in the academy have usually found it useful to classify universities as "research/international" or "teaching/local" institutions.

Globalization has made that dichotomy no longer useful for thinking about university missions and policies. It seems to me that all institutions in a nation-state are affected by globalization, thus all can be considered "local" universities for purposes of this discussion.

Perhaps the university category most dramatically affected by globalization is the institution heretofore seen as having a "sub-national" (i.e., local) mission. This is because new technologies of communication and transmission open such universities to all of the contact methodologies available to the other, more international, institutions. Not only does such technology create potential for a new mission and context for the university, it also simultaneously establishes a global role for itself in forging worldwide economic, commercial, and even political links.

To endure and thrive in the 21st century, local universities will have to be effective as a nexus of research, technological, and economic development, all of which have already become globalized.

I say *nexus*, because the college will not be the only player, will not be the research site perhaps, or the active agent of information production, receipt, or transfer. Rather, it will be the strategic venue for the communication of the experience, results of others, the venue for matching government and private sector needs for information with global capacities for providing such information.

The local university will expand its role as *entrepot* to its community for intellectual resources and technological innovations needed by the several parties for which the local university holds service obligations. Information from global sources will be shipped to the university where it will be processed and distributed; such an information market already exists and colleges must understand it and successfully operate in that market.

This implies a broader role for every local university than curricular offering and degree granting. For us in the United States, it requires the network of institutions to enable us to achieve both infrastructure adequacy and maintain institutional differentiation.

Globalization will require local universities to address the tension that has always—at least in the United States—marked the consideration of the university role as provider of economic and social responses to community needs on the one hand, and the university need to maintain some distance from the immediate, practical needs and concerns. Globalization of the environment for government and private sector entities and virtually every aspect of life for the citizen of tomorrow will perhaps exacerbate that tension.

No university—local or international—can ignore so pervasive a phenomenon as globalization. Such institutions must be alert to prepare themselves to empower their societies to be competitive in the technological world that has produced such global impact. In doing so, they will raise the intensity of global impact.

History should tell us that the rise of such change forces will give the rise to objectors to such change. The very power of globalization is sure to stimulate counter-action. Indeed, the globalization thesis in collision with its antithesis will—so Toynbee promises—produce a synthesis, which will shape the nature of academic, economic, and political relationship in the future.

Globalization, in changing the conditions for governments and corporate activity, brings pressures on local universities whose mandate is to serve those bodies. As an international fact, globalization generates some obvious challenges for nations and governments. These include the following:

1. Global Economic Challenges—"The winners in the global economy will be those who put together the world's best in design, manufacture, research, execution, and marketing on the largest scale. Rarely are all of the elements located in one country. . . . " (Jack Welch, CEO of General Electric).

Clearly, local universities will be required to play a part in responding to such economic challenge: providing skills training, workforce development, research-basic and applied, and developing global scale partnerships.

2. Global Technological Challenge—We know that the principal drive of global economic change and advancement is technology, which in turn is driven by the ever-more powerful computer.

Technology is the principal force driving change in local university organization and work.

Today, technology's major manifestation is as information and telecommunication. This will bring to the local university a new generation of students more technologically literate than most faculty today.

The US Conference Board asserts that the growing power of computers throughout the world will drive the growth of economies well into the future (as quoted by Fosler).

Of course, similar challenges to government and social entities can be expected in environmental and political policies, with consequent pressures on local universities for knowledge and professionally educated people.

National government and private sector entities need information, knowledge and analytical capacities more than ever before. Clearly, local universities will be expected to help provide them. Very likely, response by the university will lead to re-assessment of priorities and changes from the present allocation of resources of personnel and facilities.

Information technology already has a dramatic effect on how colleges and universities operate. Such technology, by its very nature, is global. We are bound together in a World Wide Web that connects us to massive amounts of knowledge. And computers give us the capacity to digest and analyze this knowledge at an equally dizzying speed.

In this environment, the distinction between global and local is blurred. Distinction between research and teaching is difficult and largely irrelevant. Small, so-called local colleges may not engage in the capital-intensive research, but instead focus on teaching. But information technology is leveling the field. More professors in more fields can conduct significant research from their local university office. Every campus will face pressures to invest in the computing and information infrastructure to enable faculty and students to access this technology. This is the most visible impact of globalization on the local university.

The local university functions and mission can be expected to be profoundly changed by the impact of globalization. As the beneficiary governments and societies of local universities have been strained an re-formed by globalization demands, so also have there occurred changes in what they require from the local universities that serve them.

The local university role in reconstruction of a market, re-entry into a new industry, re-training of managers (or workers), and re-education of citizens in economics and democratic forms of public action call for re-formations based on new fundamental principles.

Globalization will produce in the local university, the following major impacts:

1. A new orientation to the government it serves.
2. A new set of relationships for its staff within the university and between the university and the public and private sectors of the community.
3. A new sense of professional commitment by university staff to public service.
4. A new pattern of resource flow in support of university functions. Globalization can bring new relationships that open up more avenues of resources—grants, contracts, and fees for services both within the host nation-state and multi-laterally.
5. New but not the same expectations among constituent groups within the university; students, professors, clients, et al.
6. New patterns of relationships, such as partnerships and consortia with cognate institutions—institutes, clinics, universities—around the world.
7. New or greatly reformed roles for the local university in its new globalized orientations, such as:
   a. Incubator—Recognizing the social, cultural, and economic strains growing out of globalization will require testing and marketing new ideas and practices. This is likely to increase the local university functions

as laboratory for assessing the efficacy and acceptability of potential solutions. Local universities will have a strategic advantage in their position between the practical problem solving of economic life and their engagement in the life of the mind which will legitimate them as neutral incubators of new ideas about both the natural science world and the political world.

b. Mediator—The local university may be the local culture's most effective setting to mediate the demands to preserve traditional values—at least in education—and demands for new approaches to economic, technological, and social development.

8. Globalization will require expansion of the role of local university in all of the above ways and probably more, but the traditional local roles of teacher and preserver of accumulated knowledge and wisdom remain, and will continue to be vital to the stability of the local society.

In my opinion, globalization and its impacts are essentially unavoidable. The effects will be pervasive and unsettling. They will stimulate responses that will be different, reflecting the different values, history, and stability of each nation/culture involved.

Globalization cannot be stopped; it is in full stride. It can be shaped and directed to bring about maximum benefit to world societies. Of all the institutions of modern society, the academy, especially the local university may be the most effective in harnessing the energy of globalization and directing it toward locally significant ends.

Colloquia such as this are important to raise the level of consciousness of the cautions and concerns to be accommodated and the degree of preparedness by universities for the globalized environment looming ahead.

Chapter 6:

GLOBALIZATION AND THE STRATEGIC MANAGEMENT OF REGIONS

David B. Audretsch
Insitute for Development Strategies, Indiana University and Centre for Economic Policy Research, London
and A. Roy Thurik
Erasmus University, Rotterdam and EIM Research Institute, The Hague

INTRODUCTION

Perhaps one of the less-understood phenomena accompanying the increased globalization at the close of the 21st century has been a shift in the comparative advantage of high-wage countries towards knowledge-based economic activity. An important implication of this shift in this comparative advantage is that much of the production and commercialization of new economic knowledge is less associated with footloose multinational corporations and more associated with high-tech innovative regional clusters, such as Silicon Valley, Research Triangle, and Route 122. Only a few years ago the conventional wisdom predicted that globalization would render the demise of the region as a meaningful unit of economic analysis. Yet the obsession of policy-makers around the globe to "create the next Silicon Valley" reveals the increased importance of geographic proximity and regional agglomerations. The purpose of this paper is to explain why and how geography matters in a globalizing economy, which has resulted in the emergence of the strategic management, not of the firm, but of the *Standort*, or location.

GLOBALIZATION

That globalization is one of the defining changes at the turn of the century is clear from a reading of the popular press. Like all grand concepts, a definition for globalization is elusive and elicits criticism. That domestic economies are globalizing is a cliché makes it no less true. In fact, the shift in economic activity from a local or national sphere to an international or global orientation ranks among the most vehement changes shaping the current economic landscape.

The driving force underlying the emerging globalization has been technology. While there are many different aspects to the technological revolution, the advent of the microprocessor combined with its application in telecommunications has altered the economic meanings of national borders and distance.

Observing the speed at virtually no cost with which information can be transmitted across geographic space via the Internet, fax machines, and electronic communication superhighways, *The Economist* recently proclaimed on its title page, "The Death of Distance."[1] The new communications technologies have triggered a virtual spatial revolution in terms of the geography of production. According to *The Economist*, "The death of distance as a determinant of the cost of communications will probably be the single most important economic force shaping society in the first half of the next century." What the telecommunications revolution has done is to reduce the cost of transmitting information across geographic space to virtually zero. At the same time, the microprocessor revolution has made it feasible for nearly everyone to participate in global communications.

The number of Internet hosts worldwide has exploded just in the decade of the 1990s.[2] There were almost no hosts at the start of the decade and approaching ten million hosts by the end of the decade. This explosion in the Internet corresponds to a vast increase in investment in information and communication technologies. Information and communication technologies are accounting for a greater share of investment between the 1980s and 1990s in major OECD countries. A recent survey of use in higher education in the United States revealed an increasing reliance on information technologies by universities (OECD 1998). In 1995, less than two-thirds of the American campus systems were connected to an IT network; within two years, 81 percent were connected.

The advent of global telecommunications has made the interaction between individuals possible at a trivial cost. For example, international collaboration in publications in physics increased for American scientists from 8.8 percent in 1981 to 17.1 percent in 1991. International collaboration during this period doubled in physics, biology, and chemistry. Inferences about the degree of and increase in globalization based on international trade statistics miss an important point—it is the quality and not just the quantity of international transactions that have changed. Interaction among individuals adds a very different quality to the more traditional measures of trade, foreign direct investment, and capital flows—and also has very different implications for the development of economic activities. This additional quality contributed by the transnational interactions of individuals, and not just arm's-length transactions by corporations exposes people to ideas and experiences that were previously inaccessible.

Globalization would not have occurred to the degree that it has if the fundamental changes were restricted to the advent of the microprocessor and telecommunications. It took a political revolution in significant parts of the world to reap the benefits from these technological changes. The political counterpart of the technological revolution was the increase in democracy and concomitant stability in areas of the world that had previously been inaccessible. The Cold War combined with internal political instability rendered potential investments in Eastern Europe and much of the developing world as risky and impractical. During the post-war era most trade and economic investment was generally confined to Europe and North America, and later a few of the Asian countries, principally Japan and the Asian Tigers. Trade with countries behind the iron curtain was restricted and in some cases prohibited. Even trade with Japan and other Asian countries was highly regulated and restricted. Similarly, investments in politically unstable countries in South America and the Mid-East resulted in episodes of national takeovers and confiscation where the foreign investors lost their investments. Such political instability rendered foreign direct investment outside of Europe and North America to be particularly risky and of limited value.

The fall of the Berlin Wall and subsequent downfall of communism in Eastern Europe and the former Soviet Union was a catalyst for stability and accessibility to parts of the world that had previously been inaccessible for decades. Within just a few years it has become possible not just to trade with, but also to invest in countries such as Hungary, the Czech Republic, Poland, and Slovenia, as well as China, Vietnam, and Indonesia. For example, India became accessible as a trading and investment partner after opening its economy in the early 1990s. Trade and investment with the developed countries quickly blossomed. Trade and investment with the United States tripled between 1996 and 1997, reflecting the rapid change in two dimensions. First, India was confronted with sudden changes in trade and investment, not to mention a paradigmatic shift in ways of doing business. Second, to the foreign partner, in this case the United States, taking advantage of opportunities in India also meant downward pressure on wages and even plant closings in the home country.

With the opening of some of these areas and participating in the world economy for the first time in decades, the post-war equilibrium came to a sudden end. This created the opportunities associated with gaping disequilibria. Consider the large differentials in labor costs. As long as the Berlin Wall stood, and countries such as China and Vietnam remained closed, large discrepancies in wage rates could be maintained without eliciting responses in trade and foreign direct investment. The low wage rates in China or parts of the former USSR neither invited foreign companies to build plants nor resulted in large-scale trade with the west based on access to low production costs. Investment by foreign companies was either prohibited by local governments or considered to be too risky by the companies. Similarly trade and other restrictions limited the capabilities of firms in those countries from being able to produce and trade with Western nations.

Thus, the gaping wage differentials existing while the Wall stood and much of the communist world was cut off from the West were suddenly exposed in the early 1990s. There were not only unprecedented labor cost differentials but also massive and willing populations craving to join the high levels of consumption that had become the norm in Western Europe and North America.[3] For example, in the early part of the 1990s, the daily earnings of labor were estimated to be $92.24 in the United States and $78.34 in the European Union. This was a sharp contrast shortly after the Berlin Wall fell and wages were only $6.14 in Poland and $6.45 in the Czech Republic. In Asia, the wage gap was even greater, where the daily earnings were $1.53 in China, $2.46 in India and $1.25 in Sri Lanka. The potential labor force in countries like China, with 464 million workers, and India with 341 million workers dwarfs the workforce in North America and Europe.

Of course, the productivity of labor is vastly greater in the West, which compensates to a significant degree for such large wage differentials. Still, given the magnitude of these numbers both trade and investment have responded to the opportunities made possible by the events of 1989.

While the most salient feature of globalization involves interaction and interfaces among individuals across national boundaries, the more traditional measures of transnational activity reflect an upward trend of global activities. These traditional measures include trade (exports and imports), foreign direct investment (inward and outward), international capital flows, and inter-country labor mobility. The overall trend for all of these measures has been strongly positive. The trade of goods nearly tripled between 1985 and 1996. The trade of services increased by more than three times over this time period. The increases in investment income, direct investment and portfolio investment were even greater. But the increase in all of these measures within just over a decade reflects the increasing degree of globalization.

The degree of world trade, measured by exports and imports has increased over time. World exports increased from $1.3 trillion in 1970 to nearly $5 trillion in 1999, in constant dollars. While some of this increase in the world export rate is attributable to an increased participation in international trade by countries that had previously been excluded, export rates in the leading industrialized countries have also increased over the past three decades.[4] For example, US exports and imports have increased from 11 percent of GDP in 1970 to more than 25 percent by 1999.

The world volume of trade has increased by nearly 400 percent between 1970 and 1997. Over this same period global production has only doubled. In the most developed countries the increase in trade has been even greater. For example, exports as a share of gross domestic product for 49 developed countries has risen from around 18 percent in 1982 to around 25 percent by 1999. Similarly, real exports have increased in the United States from \$86.8 billion in 1960, to \$818.0 billion in 1996. At the same time, real imports have risen from \$108.1 billion to \$883.0 billion.

The increase in world trade is also not attributable to the influence of just a few industries or sectors, but rather systematic across most parts of the economy. The exposure to foreign competition in manufacturing increased by about one-sixth in the OECD countries. The exposure to foreign competition increased in every single OECD country, with the exception of Japan. In addition, it increased in most of the manufacturing industries.

A different manifestation of globalization involves foreign direct investment, which has increased by 700 percent between 1970 and 1997 for the entire world. The increase in global FDI has also not been solely the result of a greater participation by countries previously excluded from the world economy. FDI as a percentage of GDP increased in the 1970s, 1980s and 1990s for the major economies of the US and the engine of the European economy, Germany. In the US annual FDI represented slightly more than one percent of GDP during the 1970s. In the 1980s, this had risen to around 1.2 percent. By the 1990s annual FDI was more than 1.5 percent of GDP. For the United States outward foreign direct investment increased from \$1,637.1 billion in 1987 to \$2,931.9 billion in 1995. Inward foreign direct investment into the United States increased from \$1,385.9 billion to \$3,745.9 billion over this same time period.

Trans-national capital flows have also increased in the past two decades. The value of bonds and equities involved in cross-border transactions has exploded over the past two decades for the six of the largest economies. In addition, the amount of foreign exchange traded has also increased. The cross-border transactions in bonds and equities as a percentage of GDP rose in the US from 9.0 percent in 1980 to 135.5 percent by 1995. In Italy the increase was from 1.1 percent to 250.9 percent, and in Germany from 7.5 percent to 168.3 percent.

THE REGIONAL RESPONSE

Confronted with lower cost competition in foreign locations, producers in the high-cost countries have three options apart from doing nothing and losing global market share: (1) reduce wages and other production costs sufficiently to compete with the low-cost foreign producers, (2) substitute equipment and technology for labor to increase productivity, and (3) shift production out of the high-cost location and into the low-cost location.

Many of the European and American firms that have successfully restructured resorted to the last two alternatives. Substituting capital and technology for labor, along with shifting production to lower-cost locations has resulted in waves of *Corporate Downsizing* throughout Europe and North America. At the same time, it has generally preserved the viability of many of the large corporations. As record levels of both European and American stock indexes indicate, the companies have not generally suffered. For example, between 1979 and 1995 more than 43 million jobs were lost in the United States as a result of corporate downsizing.[5] This includes 24.8 million blue-collar jobs and 18.7 million white-collar jobs. Similarly, the 500 largest US manufacturing corporations cut 4.7 million jobs between 1980 and 1993, or one-quarter of their work force.[6] Perhaps most disconcerting, the rate of corporate downsizing has apparently increased over time in the United States, even as the unemployment rate has fallen. During most of the 1980s, about one in 25 workers lost a job. In the 1990s this has risen to one in 20 workers.

This wave of corporate downsizing has triggered cries of betrayal and lack of social conscience on the part of the large corporations.[7] But it is a mistake to blame the corporations for this wave of downsizing that has triggered massive job losses and rising unemployment in so many countries. These corporations are simply trying to survive in an economy of global competitors who have access to lower cost inputs.

Much of the policy debate responding to the twin forces of the telecommunications revolution and increased globalisation has revolved around a trade-off between maintaining higher wages but suffering greater unemployment versus higher levels of employment but at the cost of lower wage rates. There is, however, an alternative. It does not require sacrificing wages to create new jobs, nor does it require fewer jobs to maintain wage levels and the social safety net. This alternative involves shifting economic activity out of the traditional industries where the high-cost countries of Europe and North America have lost the comparative advantage and into those industries where the comparative advantage is compatible with both high wages and high levels of employment—knowledge-based economic activity.

Globalization has rendered the comparative advantage in traditional moderate technology industries incompatible with high wage levels. At the same time, the emerging comparative advantage that is compatible with high wage levels is based on innovative activity. For example, employment has increased by 15 percent in Silicon Valley between 1992 and 1996, even though the mean income is 50 percent greater than in the rest of the country.[8]

Thus, the regional response to globalization has been the emergence of strategic management policy—not for firms, but for regions. As long as corporations were inextricably linked to their regional location by substantial sunk costs, such as capital investment, the competitiveness of a region was identical to the competitiveness of the corporations located in that region. A quarter-century ago, while the proclamation, "What is good for General Motors is good for America" may have been controversial, few would have disagreed that "What is good for General Motors is good for Detroit." And so it was with US Steel in Pittsburgh and Volkswagen in Wolfsburg. As long as the corporation thrived, so would the region.

As globalization has rendered not only the degree to which the traditional economic factors of capital and labor are sunk, but also shifted the comparative advantage in the high-wage countries of North America and Europe toward knowledge-based economic activity, corporations have been forced to shift production to lower-cost locations. This has led to a delinking between the competitiveness of firms and regions. The advent of the strategic management of regions has been a response to the realization that the strategic management of corporations includes a policy option not available to regions—changing the production *Standort*.

At the heart of the strategic management of regions has been the development and enhancement of factors of production that cannot be transferred across geographic space at low cost—principally, although not exclusively, knowledge and ideas.

That knowledge spills over is barely disputed. In disputing the importance of knowledge externalities in explaining the geographic concentration of economic activity, Krugman (1991) and others do not question the existence or importance of such knowledge spillovers. In fact, they argue that such knowledge externalities are so important and forceful that there is no compelling reason for a geographic boundary to limit the spatial extent of the spillover. According to this line of thinking, the concern is not that knowledge does not spill over but that it should stop spilling over just because it hits a geographic border, such as a city limit, state line, or national boundary. As illustrated by the title page of *The Economist* proclaiming "The Death of Distance,"[9] the claim that geographic location is important to the process linking knowledge spillovers to innovative activity in a world of e-mail, fax machines, and cyberspace may seem surprising and even paradoxical. The resolution to the paradox posed by the localisation of knowledge spillovers in an era where the telecommunications revolution has drastically reduced the cost of communication lies in a distinction between knowledge and information. *Information*, such as the price of gold on the New York Stock Exchange, or the value of the Yen in London, can be easily codified and has a singular meaning and interpretation. By contrast, *knowledge* is vague, difficult to codify, and often only serendipitously recognised. While the marginal cost of transmitting information across geographic space has been rendered invariant by the telecommunications revolution, the marginal cost of transmitting knowledge, and especially tacit knowledge, rises with distance.

Von Hipple (1994) demonstrates that high-context, uncertain knowledge, or what he terms as "sticky" knowledge, is best transmitted via face-to-face interaction and through frequent and repeated contact. Geographic proximity matters in transmitting knowledge, because as Kenneth Arrow (1962) pointed out some three decades ago, such tacit knowledge is inherently non-rival in nature, and knowledge developed for any particular application can easily spill over and have economic value in very different applications. As Glaeser, Kallal, Scheinkman. and Shleifer (1992: p. 1126) have observed, "intellectual breakthroughs must cross hallways and streets more easily than oceans and continents."

The importance of local proximity for the transmission of knowledge spillovers has been observed in many different contexts. It has been pointed out that, "business is a social activity, and you have to be where important work is taking place."[10] A survey of nearly 1,000 executives located in America's 60 largest metropolitan areas ranked Raleigh/Durham as the best city for knowledge workers and for innovative activity.[11] The reason is that "A lot of brainy types who made their way to Raleigh/Durham were drawn by three top research universities . . . US businesses, especially those whose success depends on staying at the top of new technologies and processes, increasingly want to be where hot new ideas are percolating. A presence in brain-power centers like Raleigh/Durham pays off in new products and new ways of doing business. Dozens of small biotechnology and software operations are starting up each year and growing like *kudzu* in the fertile climate."[12]

Not only did Krugman (1991: p. 53) doubt that knowledge spillovers are not geographically constrained but he also argued that they were impossible to measure because "knowledge flows are invisible, they leave no paper trail by which they may be measured and tracked." However, an emerging literature (Jaffe, Trajtenberg, and Henderson 1993) has overcome data constraints to measure the extent of knowledge spillovers and link them to the geography of innovative activity. Jaffe (1989), Feldman (1994), and Audretsch and Feldman (1996) modified the model of the knowledge production function to include an explicit specification for both the spatial and product dimensions:

$$I_{si} = IRD^{\beta 1} * (UR_{si})^{\beta 1} * [UR_{si} * (GC_{si})^{\beta 3}] * \varepsilon_{si} \qquad (1)$$

where I is innovative output, IRD is private corporate expenditures on R&D, UR is the research expenditures undertaken at universities, and GC measures the geographic coincidence between university and corporate research. The unit of observation for estimation is at the spatial level, s, a state, and industry level, i. Jaffe (1989) used the number of inventions registered with the United States patent office as a measure of innovative activity. By contrast, Audretsch and Feldman (1996) and Acs, Audretsch, and Feldman (1992) developed a direct measure of innovative output consisting of new product introductions.

Estimation of equation (1) essentially shifts the model of the knowledge production function from the unit of observation of a firm to that of a geographic unit. The consistent empirical evidence that $\beta_1 \geq 0$, $\beta_2 \geq 0$, $\beta_3 \geq 0$ supports the notion knowledge spills over for third-party use from university research laboratories as well as industry R&D laboratories. This empirical evidence suggests that location and proximity clearly matter in exploiting knowledge spillovers. Not only have Jaffe, Trajtenberg, and Henderson (1993) found that patent citations tend to occur more frequently within the state in which they were patented than outside of that state, but Audretsch and Feldman (1996) found that the propensity of innovative activity to cluster geographically tends to be greater in industries where new economic knowledge plays a more important role. Prevenzer (1997) and Zucker, Darby, and Armstrong (1994) show that in biotechnology, which is an industry based almost exclusively on new knowledge, the firms tend to cluster together in just a handful of locations. This finding is supported by Audretsch and Stephan (1996) who examine the geographic relationships of scientists working with biotechnology firms. The importance of geographic proximity is clearly shaped by the role played by the scientist. The scientist is more likely to be located in the same region as the firm when the relationship involves the transfer of new economic knowledge. However, when the scientist is providing a service to the company that does not involve knowledge transfer, local proximity becomes much less important.

There is reason to believe that knowledge spillovers are not homogeneous across firms. In estimating Equation (1) for large and small enterprises separately, Acs, Audretsch, and Feldman (1994) provide some insight into the puzzle posed by the recent wave of studies identifying vigorous innovative activity emanating from small firms in certain industries. How are these small, and frequently new, firms able to generate innovative output while undertaking generally negligible amounts of investment into knowledge generating inputs, such as R&D? The answer appears to be through exploiting knowledge created by expenditures on research in universities and on R&D in large corporations. Their findings suggest that the innovative output of all firms rises along with an increase in the amount of R&D inputs, both in private corporations as well as in university laboratories. However, R&D expenditures made by private companies play a particularly important role in providing knowledge inputs to the innovative activity of large firms, while expenditures on research made by universities serve as an especially key input for generating innovative activity in small enterprises. Apparently, large firms are more adept at exploiting knowledge created in their own laboratories, while their smaller counterparts have a comparative advantage at exploiting spillovers from university laboratories.

A conceptual problem arises with economies accruing to the knowledge transmission associated with agglomeration. Once a city, region, or state develops a viable cluster of production and innovative activity why should it ever lose the first-mover advantage? One answer, provided by Audretsch and Feldman (1996) is that the relative importance of local proximity and therefore agglomeration effects is shaped by the stage of the industry lifecycle. A growing literature suggests that who innovates and how much innovative activity is undertaken is closely linked to the phase of the industry lifecycle (Klepper 1996). Audretsch and Feldman (1996) argue that an additional key aspect to the evolution of innovative activity over the industry lifecycle is *where* that innovative activity takes place. The theory of knowledge spillovers, derived from the knowledge production function, suggests that the propensity for innovative activity to cluster spatially will be the greatest in industries where tacit knowledge pays an important role. As argued above, it is *tacit knowledge*, as opposed to *information* that can only be transmitted informally, and typically demands direct and repeated contact. The role of tacit knowledge in generating innovative activity is presumably the greatest during the early stages of the industry lifecycle, before product standards have been established and a dominant design has emerged. Audretsch and Feldman (1996) classify 210 industries into four different stages of the lifecycle. The results provide considerable evidence suggesting that the propensity for innovative activity to spatially cluster is shaped by the stage of the industry lifecycle. On the one hand, new economic knowledge embodied in skilled workers tends to raise the propensity for innovative activity to spatially cluster throughout all phases of the industry lifecycle. On the other hand, certain other sources of new economic knowledge, such as university research, tend to elevate the propensity for innovative activity to cluster during the introduction stage of the lifecycle, but not during the growth stage, and then again during the stage of decline.

Perhaps most striking is the finding that greater geographic concentration of production actually leads to more, and not less, dispersion of innovative activity. Apparently, innovative activity is promoted by knowledge spillovers that occur within a distinct geographic region, particularly in the early stages of the industry lifecycle, but as the industry evolves toward maturity and decline may be dispersed by additional increases in concentration of production that have been built up within that same region. The evidence suggests that what may serve as an agglomerating influence in triggering innovative activity to spatially cluster during the introduction and growth stages of the industry lifecycle, may later result in a congestion effect, leading to greater dispersion in innovative activity. While the literature on economic geography has traditionally focused on factors such as rents, commuting time, and pollution as constituting congestion and dissipating agglomeration economies (Henderson 1986), this type of congestion refers to lock-in with respect to new ideas. While there may have been agglomeration economies in automobiles in Detroit in the 1970 and computers in the Northeast Corridor in the 1980s, a type of intellectual lock-in made it difficult for Detroit to shift out of large-car production and for IBM and DEC to shift out of mainframe computers and into mini-computers. Perhaps it was this type of intellectual congestion that led to the emergence of the personal computer in California, about as far away from the geographic agglomeration of the mainframe computer as is feasible on the mainland of the United States. Even when IBM developed its own personal computer, the company located its fledgling PC facility in Boca Raton, Florida, way outside of the mainframe agglomeration, in the Northeast Corridor. Thus, there is at least some evidence suggesting that spatial agglomerations, just as other organisational units of economic activity are vulnerable to technological lock-in, with the result being in certain circumstances that new ideas need new space.

THE EMERGENCE OF ENTREPRENEURSHIP

That SMEs would emerge as becoming more important seems to be contrary to many of the conventional theories of innovation. The starting point for most theories of innovation is the firm. In such theories the firms are exogenous and their performance in generating technological change is endogenous (Arrow 1962). For example, in the most prevalent model found in the literature of technological change, the model of the knowledge production function, formalised by Zvi Griliches (1979), firms exist exogenously and then engage in the pursuit of new economic knowledge as an input into the process of generating innovative activity. The most decisive input in the knowledge production function is new economic knowledge. Knowledge as an input in a production function is inherently different than the more traditional inputs of labour, capital, and land. While the economic value of the traditional inputs is relatively certain, knowledge is intrinsically uncertain and its potential value is asymmetric across economic agents.[14] The most important, although not the only source of new knowledge is considered to be research and development (R&D). Other key factors generating new economic knowledge include a high degree of human capital, a skilled labour force, and a high presence of scientists and engineers.

There is considerable empirical evidence supporting the model of the knowledge production function. This empirical link between knowledge inputs and innovative output apparently becomes stronger as the unit of observation becomes increasingly aggregated. For example, at the unit of observation of countries, the relationship between R&D and patents is very strong. The most innovative countries, such as the United States, Japan, and Germany, also tend to undertake high investments in R&D. By contrast, little patent activity is associated with developing countries, which have very low R&D expenditures. Similarly, the link between R&D and innovative output, measured in terms of either patents or new product innovations is also very strong when the unit of observation is the industry. The most innovative industries, such as computers, instruments, and pharmaceuticals also tend to be the most R&D intensive. Audretsch (1995) finds a simple correlation coefficient of 0.74 between R&D inputs and innovative output at the level of four-digit standard industrial classification (SIC) industries. However, when the knowledge production function is tested for the unit of observation of the firm, the link between knowledge inputs and innovative output becomes either tenuous and weakly positive in some studies and even non-existent or negative in others. The model of the knowledge production function becomes particularly weak when small firms are included in the sample. This is not surprising, since formal R&D is concentrated among the largest corporations, but a series of studies (Acs and Audretsch 1990) has clearly documented that small firms account for a disproportional share of new product innovations given their low R&D expenditures.

The breakdown of the knowledge production function at the level of the firm raises the question, *Where do innovative firms with little or no R&D get the knowledge inputs?* This question becomes particularly relevant for small and new firms that undertake little R&D themselves, yet contribute considerable innovative activity in newly emerging industries such as biotechnology and computer software (Audretsch 1995). One answer that has recently emerged in the economics literature is from other, third-party firms or research institutions, such as universities. Economic knowledge may spill over from the firm conducting the R&D or the research laboratory of a university

Why should knowledge spill over from the source of origin? At least two major channels or mechanisms for knowledge spillovers have been identified in the literature. Both of these spillover mechanisms revolve around the issue of appropriability of new knowledge. Cohen and Levinthal (1989) suggest that firms develop the capacity to adapt new technology and ideas developed in other firms and are therefore able to appropriate some of the returns accruing to investments in new knowledge made externally.

By contrast, Audretsch (1995) proposes shifting the unit of observation away from exogenously assumed firms to individuals, such as scientists, engineers, or other knowledge workers—agents with endowments of new economic knowledge. When the lens is shifted away from the firm to the individual as the relevant unit of observation, the appropriability issue remains, but the question becomes, *How can economic agents with a given endowment of new knowledge best appropriate the returns from that knowledge?* If the scientist or engineer can pursue the new idea within the organizational structure of the firm developing the knowledge and appropriate roughly the expected value of that knowledge, he has no reason to leave the firm. On the other hand, if he places a greater value on his ideas than do the decision-making bureaucracy of the incumbent firm, he may choose to start a new firm to appropriate the value of his knowledge. In the metaphor provided by Albert O. Hirschman (1970), if voice proves to be ineffective within incumbent organisations, and loyalty is sufficiently weak, a knowledge worker may resort to exit the firm or university where the knowledge was created in order to form a new company. In this spillover channel the knowledge production function is actually reversed. The knowledge is exogenous and embodied in a worker. The firm is created endogenously in the worker's effort to appropriate the value of his knowledge through innovative activity.

What emerges from the new evolutionary theories and empirical evidence on innovation as a competitive strategy deployed by SMEs is that markets are in motion, with a lot of new firms entering the industry and a lot of firms exiting out of the industry. But is this motion horizontal, in that the bulk of firms exiting are comprised of firms that had entered relatively recently, or vertical, in that a significant share of the exiting firms had been established incumbents that were displaced by younger firms? In trying to shed some light on this question, Audretsch (1995) proposes two different models of the evolutionary process of industries over time. Some industries can be best characterized by the model of the conical revolving door, where new businesses are started, but there is also a high propensity to subsequently exit from the market. Other industries may be better characterized by the metaphor of the forest, where incumbent establishments are displaced by new entrants. Which view is more applicable apparently depends on three major factors—the underlying technological conditions, scale economies, and demand. Where scale economies play an important role, the model of the revolving door seems to be more applicable. While the rather starting result that the startup and entry of new businesses is apparently not deterred by the presence of high-scale economies, a process of firm selection analogous to a revolving door ensures that only those establishments successful enough to grow will be able to survive beyond more than a few years. Thus the bulk of new entrants that are not so successful ultimately exit within a few years subsequent to entry.

When SMEs deploy a strategy of innovation, they typically start at a very small scale of output. They are motivated by the desire to appropriate the expected value of new economic knowledge. But, depending upon the extent of scale economies in the industry, the firm may not be able to remain viable indefinitely at its startup size. Rather, if scale economies are anything other than negligible, the new firm is likely to have to grow to survive. The temporary survival of new firms is presumably supported through the deployment of a strategy of compensating factor differentials that enables the firm to discover whether or not it has a viable product.

The empirical evidence has found that the post-entry growth of firms that survive tends to be spurred by the extent to which there is a gap between the MES level of output and the size of the firm. However, the likelihood of any particular new firm surviving tends to decrease as this gap increases. Such new SMEs deploying a strategy of innovation to attain competitiveness are apparently engaged in the selection process. Only those SMEs offering a viable product that can be produced efficiently will grow and ultimately approach or attain the MES level of output. The remainder will stagnate, and depending upon the severity of the other selection mechanism—the extent of scale economies—may ultimately be forced to exit out of the industry. Thus, in highly innovative industries, there is a continuing process of the entry of new SMEs into industries and not necessarily the permanence of individual SMEs over the long run. Although the skewed size distribution of firms persists with remarkable stability over long periods of time, a constant set of SMEs does not appear to be responsible for this skewed distribution. Rather, by serving as agents of change, SMEs provide an essential source of new ideas and experimentation that otherwise would remain untapped in the economy.

CONCLUSIONS

Globalization is shifting the comparative advantage in the OECD countries away from being based on traditional inputs of production, such as land, labor, and capital, toward knowledge. As the comparative advantage has become increasingly based on new knowledge, public policy has responded in two fundamental ways. The first has been to shift the policy focus away from the traditional triad of policy instruments essentially constraining the freedom of firms to contract—regulation, competition policy, or antitrust in the US, and public ownership of business. The policy approach of constraint was sensible as long as the major issue was how to restrain large corporations in possession of considerable market power. That this policy is less relevant in a global economy is reflected by the waves of deregulation and privatisation throughout the OECD. Instead, a new policy approach is emerging which focuses on enabling the creation and commercialisation of knowledge. Examples of such policies include encouraging R&D, venture capital, and new-firm startups. In particular, the new focus of SME policies is to promote the first type of strategy deployed by SMEs to enhance global competitiveness—innovation. Probably the greatest and most salient shift in SME policy over the last 15 years has been a shift from trying to preserve SMEs that are confronted with a cost disadvantage due to size inherent scale disadvantages, toward promoting the startup and viability of SMEs involved in the commercialization of knowledge, or knowledge-based SMEs.

For example, the United States Congress enacted the Small Business Innovation Research (SBIR) program in the early 1980s as a response to the loss of American competitiveness in global markets. Congress mandated each federal agency with allocating around 4 percent of its annual budget to funding innovative small firms as a mechanism for restoring American international competitiveness. The SBIR provides a mandate to the major R&D agencies in the United States to allocate a share of the research budget to innovative small firms. Last year the SBIR program amounted to around $1.2 billion. The SBIR consists of three phases. Phase I is oriented toward determining the scientific and technical merit along with the feasibility of a proposed research idea. A Phase I award provides an opportunity for a small business to establish the feasibility and technical merit of a proposed innovation. The duration of the award is six months and cannot exceed $70,000. Phase II extends the technological idea and emphasizes commercialization. A Phase II Award is granted to only the most promising of the Phase I projects based on scientific/technical merit, the expected value to the funding agency, company capability, and commercial potential. The duration of the award is a maximum of 24 months and generally does not exceed $600,000. Approximately 40 percent of the Phase I Awards continue on to Phase II. Phase III involves additional private funding for the commercial application of a technology. A Phase III Award is for the infusion and use of a product into the commercial market. Private sector investment, in various forms, is typically present in Phase III. Under the Small Business Research and Development Enhancement Act of 1992, funding in Phase I was increased to $100,000, and in Phase II to $750,000.

The SBIR represents about 60 percent of all public SME finance programs. Taken together, the public SME finance is about two-thirds as large as private venture capital. In 1995, the sum of equity financing provided through and guaranteed by public programs financing SMEs was $2.4 billion, which amounted to more than 60 percent of the total funding disbursed by traditional venture funds in that year. Equally as important, the emphasis on SBIR and most public funds is on early stage finance, which is generally ignored by private venture capital. Some of the most innovative American companies received early stage finance from SBIR, including Apple Computer, Chiron, Compaq, and Intel. Through the Small Business Innovation Research (SBIR) program, the National Institute of Health (NIH) awarded $266 million in grants to small firms for medical and biopharmaceutical research. It is expected that the SBIR program at NIH will exceed $300 million in 1999.

In addition to the NIH, the United States Department of Defense also uses the SBIR program to fund biotechnology firms. Between 1983 and 1997, there was more than $240 million in SBIR awards for biotechnology companies from the Department of Defense. Phase I accounted for $47 million and Phase II accounted for $194 million.

The benefits of the SBIR extends beyond the impact on the individual recipient firm. The social rate of return, which incorporates this external positive impact, exceeds the positive rate of return. There was no evidence of a negative rate of return associated with the SBIR. There is compelling evidence that the SBIR program has had a positive impact on developing the US biotechnology industry. The benefits have been documented as:

- The survival and growth rates of SBIR recipients have exceeded those of firms not receiving SBIR funding
- The SBIR induces scientists involved in biomedical research to change their career paths. By applying the scientific knowledge to commercialization, these scientists shift their career trajectories away from basic research toward entrepreneurship.
- The SBIR awards provide a source of funding for scientists to launch start-up firms that otherwise would not have had access to alternative sources of funding.
- SBIR awards have a powerful demonstration effect. Scientists commercializing research results by starting companies induce colleagues to consider applications and the commercial potential of their own research.

Indirect promotion of new technology-based firms (NTBFs) by the federal government has risen from 45.9 million DM in 1991 to almost 82 million DM in 1993 (BMBF 1996: p. 97). Similarly, Sternberg (1996) has shown that a number of government-sponsored technology policies have triggered the startup of new firms. The majority of the startup programs are targeted toward eliminated particular bottlenecks in the development and financing of new firms. Sternberg (1990) examines the impact that 70 innovation centers have had on the development of technology-based small firms. He finds that the majority of the entrepreneurs find a number of advantages from locating at an innovation center. The Kreditanstalt fuer Wiederaufbau (KfW), or German Reconstruction Bank, has been one of the most important institutions promoting SMEs in Germany. The KfW provides financial support for around 20,000 SMEs each year. Of these firms, 80 percent have sales less than 10 million DM. The support of SMEs by the KfW resulted in the creation of nearly 150,000 jobs in 1992 and 40,000 jobs in 1995. Similarly, the Bundesministerium fuer Bildung, Wissenschaft, Forschung und Technologie (BMBF) has had a series of programs to promote German SMEs.

The second fundamental shift involves the locus of such enabling policies, which are increasingly at the state, regional, or even local level The downsizing of federal agencies charged with the regulation of business in many of the OECD countries has been interpreted by many scholars as the eclipse of government intervention. But to interpret deregulation, privatisation, and the increased irrelevance of competition policies as the end of government intervention in business ignores an important shift in the locus and target of public policy. The last decade has seen the emergence of a broad spectrum of enabling policy initiatives that fall outside of the jurisdiction of the traditional regulatory agencies. Sternberg (1996) documents how the success of a number of different high-technology clusters spanning a number of developed countries is the direct result of enabling policies, such as the provision of venture capital or research support. For example, the Advanced Research Program in Texas has provided support for basic research and the strengthening of the infrastructure of the University of Texas, which has played a central role in developing a high-technology cluster around Austin (Feller 1997). The Thomas Edison Centers in Ohio, the Advanced Technology Centers in New Jersey, and the Centers for Advanced Technology at Case Western Reserve University, Rutgers University, and the University of Rochester have supported generic, precompetitive research. This support has generally provided diversified technology development involving a mix of activities encompassing a broad spectrum of industrial collaborators.

There is evidence that the amount of venture capital available to new-firm startups in high-technology industries in Germany is dramatically increasing. The amount of venture capital provided by direct-investment and venture capital programs sponsored by the Federal Ministry for Education, Science, Research and Technology (BMBF) has increased from about 10 million DM in 1989 to more than 458 million DM in 1997 (BMBF 1996).

One of the most interesting examples of the strategic management of regions involves the establishment of five EXIST regions in Germany, where startups from universities and government research laboratories are encouraged (BMBF 2000). The program has the explicit goals of (1) creating an entrepreneurial culture, (2) the commercialization of scientific knowledge, and (3) increasing the number of innovative start-ups and SMEs. Five regions were selected among many applicants for START funding. These are the (1) Rhein-Ruhr region (bizeps program), (2) Dresden (Dresden exists), (3) Thueringen (GET UP), (4) Karlsruhe (KEIM), and (5) Stuttgart (PUSH!).

These programs promoting entrepreneurship in a regional context are typical of the strategic management of regions. While these regional policies are clearly evolving, they are clearly gaining in importance and impact in the overall portfolio of economic policy instruments.

NOTES

[1]"The Death of Distance," *The Economist*, 30 September 1995.

[2]"Indicator Data Sources," in The New Economy Index, <http://www.dlcppi.org/ppi.org/ppi/tech/neweconomy_site/sources.html> (access June 1999)

[3]The data are adopted from Jensen (1993).

[4]"Markets Go Global," *The Economist*, 20 September 1997.

[5]"The Downsizing of America," *New York Times*, 3 March 1996, p. 1.

[6]See Audretsch (1995).

[7]As the German newspaper, *Die Zeit* (2 February, 1996, p. 1) pointed out in a front page article, "When Profits Lead to Ruin—More Profits and More Unemployment: Where is the Social Responsibility of the Firms?" the German public has responded to the recent waves of corporate downsizing with accusations that corporate Germany is no longer fulfilling its share of the social contract.

[8]"The Valley of Money's Delights," *The Economist*, 29 March, 1997, special section, p. 1.

[9]"The Death of Distance," Ibid.

[10]"The Best Cities for Knowledge Workers," *Fortune*, 15 November, 1993, p. 44.

[11]The survey was carried out in 1993 by the management consulting firm of Moran, Stahl & Boyer of New York City.

[12]"The Best Cities for Knowledge Workers," ibid.

[13]Arrow (1962) pointed out this is one of the reasons for inherent market failure.

REFERENCES

Arrow, K. 1962. "Economic Welfare and the Allocation of Resources for Invention," in R. Nelson (Ed.), *The Rate and Direction of Inventive Activity*, Princeton: Princeton University Press.

Audretsch, D. 1995. *Innovation and Industry Evolution*, Cambridge, MA: MIT Press.

———. 1998. "Agglomeration and the Location of Innovative Activity," *Oxford Review of Economic Policy*, 14(2), 18-29.

——— and Feldman, M. 1996. "R&D Spillovers and the Geography of Innovation and Production," *American Economic Review*, 86(4), 253–273.

——— and Stephan, P. 1996. "Company-Scientist Locational Links: The Case of Biotechnology," *American Economic Review*, 86(4), 641–652.

——— and A. Thurik. 1999. *Innovation, Industry Evolution and Employment*, Cambridge: Cambridge University Press.

Baptista, R.(1997. *An Empirical Study of Innovation, Entry and Diffusion in Industrial Clusters*, Ph.D. Dissertation at the University of London (London Business School).

Berman, Eli, John Bound, and Stephen Machin 1997. "Implications of Skill-Biased Technological Change: International Evidence," working paper 6166, National Bureau of Economic Research (NBER), Cambridge, MA.

Braunerhjelm, Pontus and Bo Carlsson. 1999. "Industry Clusters in Ohio and Sweden, 1975-1995," *Small Business Economics*, 12(4), June, 279–293.

Cohen, W. and Levinthal, D. 1989. 'Innovation and Learning: The Two Faces of R&D," *Economic Journal*, 99(3), 569–596.

Cooke, Philip and David Wills. 1999. "Small Firms, Social Capital and the Enhancement of Business Performance through Innovation Programmes," *Small Business Economics*, 13(3), November, 219–234.

Dunning, J.H.,1996. "The Geographical Sources of *Competitiveness of Firms: The Results of a New Survey," Transnational* Corporations, 5(3), December 1–30.

Dunning, J.H. 1998. "The Changing Geography of Foreign Direct Investment," in K. Kumar (Ed.), *Internationalization, Foreign Direct Investment and Technology Transfer: Impact and Prospects for Developing Countries*," London: Routledge.

Ellsion, G. and Glaeser, E. 1997. "Geographic Concentration in US Manufacturing Industries: A Dartboard Approach," *Journal of Political Economy*, (4), 889–927.

Feldman, M. 1994). "Knowledge Complementarity and Innovation," *Small Business Economics*, 6(3), 363–372.

——. 1994. *The Geography of Innovation*, Boston: Kluwer.

—— and Audretsch, D. 1999. "Science-Based Diversity, Specialization, Localized Competition and Innovation," *European Economic Review*, 43, 409–429.

Feller, I. 1997. "Federal and State Government Roles in Science and Technology," *Economic Development Quarterly*, 11(4), 283–296.

Glaeser, E., H. Kallal, J. Scheinkman, and A. Shleifer. 1992. "Growth of Cities," *Journal of Political Economy*, 100, 1126–1152.

Glasmeier, Amy. 1991. "Technological Discontinuities and Flexible Production Networks," *Research Policy*, 469–485.

Griliches, Z. 1979. "Issues in Assessing the Contribution of R&D to Productivity Growth," *Bell Journal of Economics*, 10, 92–116.

——. 1992. "The Search for R&D Spill-Overs," *Scandinavian Journal of Economics*, 94, 29–47.

Henderson, V. 1986. "Efficiency of Resource Usage and City Size," *Journal of Urban Economics*, 19(1), 47–70.

Henderson, Vernon (1994), "Externalities and Industrial Development," NBER Working Paper 4730, May.

——, Ari Kuncoro, and Matt Turner. 1995. "Industrial Development in Cities," *Journal of Political Economy*, 103(5), October, 1067-1090.

Hirschman, A.O. 1970. *Exit, Voice, and Loyalty*, Cambridge, MA: Harvard University Press.

Jacobs, J. 1969. *The Economy of Cities*, New York: Random House.

Jaffe, A. 1989. "Real Effects of Academic Research," *American Economic Review*, 79, 957–970.

——, M. Trajtenberg, and R. Henderson. 1993. "Geographic Localization of Knowledge Spillovers as Evidenced by Patent Citations," *Quarterly Journal of Economics*, 63, 577–598.

Kindleberger, C.P. and D.B. Audretsch. 1983. *The Multinational Corporation in the 1980s*, Cambridge: MIT Press.

Klepper, S. 1996. "Entry, Exit, Growth, and Innovation over the Product Life Cycle," *American Economic Review*, 86(4), 562–583.

Kortum, S. and J. Lerner. 1997. "Stronger Protection or Technological Revolution: What is Behind the Recent Surge in Patenting?" working paper 6204, National Bureau of Economic Research (NBER), Cambridge,MA.

Markusen, A. 1996. "Sticky Places in Slippery Space: A Typology of Industrial Districts," Economic Geography, 72(3), 293–313.

Porter, M. 1990. *The Comparative Advantage of Nations*, New York: Free Press.

Porter, Michael E. 2000. "Clusters and Government Policy," *Wirtschaftspolitische Blaetter*, 47(2), 144–154.

Prevenzer, M. 1997. "The Dynamics of Industrial Clustering in Biotechnology," *Small Business Economics*, 9(3), 255–271.

Saxenian, A. 1990. "Regional Networks and the Resurgence of Silicon Valley," *California Management Review*, 33, 89–111.

Sternberg, R. 1996. "Technology Policies and the Growth of Regions," *Small Business Economics*, 8(2), 75–86.

Stough, Roger R., Kingsley E. Haynes, and Harrison S. Campbell Jr., 1998, "Small Business Entrepreneurship in the High Technology Services Sector: An Assessment for the Edge Cities of the US National Capital Region," *Small Business Economics*, 10(1), 61–74.

Venables, A.J. 1996. 'Localization of Industry and Trade Performance," *Oxford Review of Economic Policy*, 12(3), 52–60.

Von Hipple, E. 1994. "Sticky Information and the Locus of Problem Solving: Implications for Innovation," *Management Science*, 40, 429–439.

Zucker, L., M. Darby, and J. Armstrong. 1994. '"Intellectual Capital and the Firm: The Technology of Geographically Localized Knowledge Spillovers," National Bureau of Economic Research Working Paper No. 9496, December.

Chapter 7:

LIVING APART TOGETHER IN EUROPE

Jean-Pierre van Aubel and Frans K.M. van Nispen
Department of Public Administration, Erasmus University, Rotterdam, The Netherlands

INTRODUCTION

A decade ago Alice Rivlin issued a new book in which she calls for a revival of the American dream that is "a democratic political system in which most people feel that they can affect public decisions and elect officials who will speak for them" (Rivlin 1992: p. 1). The original idea had faded due to a process of centralization. In the early days of *dual* federalism, both levels of government were relatively small, but the power was with the states (1789–1933). The activities of both government levels expanded during the depression years, but the federal government expanded more than did the states, creating a situation of *cooperative* federalism (1933–1980). The drive for centralization peaked in the early '80s and power began to shift back to the states, generating a system of *competitive* federalism (Shannon and Kee 1989). Rivlin calls for a division of the national and state responsibilities, though two previous attempts to sort these out under the label of new federalism failed (Rivlin 1992: pp. 82–84).

In the spring of 2000, Joschka Fischer, the German minister of Foreign Affairs articulated his European dream, calling for a specification of the "Finalität," that is the ultimate goal of the process of European integration. It came at a moment when Europe is challenged by two conflicting developments—globalization and localization—labeled by Tom Courchene as "glocalization" (Watts 1994).

THE EUROPEAN DREAM

The Federalism word is back after ten years ago when, after September 30, 1991, a proposal by the Dutch presidency for the creation of a political union was turned down by the other member states. Fischer, speaking personally at the Humboldt Universität in Berlin, has launched a plea for the establishment of a political union modeled on the German federation. He envisions a three-staged program. The first step in the direction of a federation should be an intensification of the cooperation between the European member states, by the creation of a group of front-runners called "Européens de l'euro," sharing a more-or-less similar view on the ultimate goal of the process of European integration:

> La seule option réaliste, alors, est que l'integration soit réalisée par les pays qui en ont la volonté politique et dont les conditions économiques et sociales sont presque identiques. En ce moment, tous ces pays appartiennent à la zone euro, dont la population dépasse déjà celles des Etats-Unis (Giscard d'Estaing and Schmidt 2000).

The establishment of a "gravity-center" should comprise the second step, leading to a European constitution, a president elected by the population, a government, and a strong parliament of two chambers (Fischer 2000a):

> Ein möglicher Zwischenschritt hin zur Vollendung der politischen Union könnte dann später die Bildung eines Gravitationszentrum sein. Eine solche Staatengruppe würde einen neuen europäischen Grund-vertrag schließen, den Nukleus einer Verfassung der Föderation. Und auf der Basis dieses Grundvertrages würde sie sich eigene Institutionen geben, eine Regierung, die innerhalb der EU in möglichst vielen Fragen für die Mitglieder der Gruppe mit einer Stimme sprechen sollte, ein starkes Parlament, einen direkt gewählten Präsidenten. Ein solches Gravitationszentrum müsste die Avantgarde, die Lokomotive für die Vollendung der politischen Integration sein und bereits alle Elemente der späteren Föderation umfassen (Fischer 2000a).

The third step should complete the process of integration by the establishment of a European federation. In a speech for an audience of students at Georgetown University in Washington, he underscored once again that confederation (read: intergovernmental cooperation) could not work in a European Union with 25 to 30 member states (Fischer 2000b).

Surprisingly, the Fischer's speech triggered hardly any debate in the other member states, with the clear exception of France who, after all, has the most to lose because Brussels may be seen as an appendage of Paris and of the French political élite (Siedentop 2000: p. 113). Fischer was counter-balanced by French President Jacques Chirac during a television interview. At face value he seems to agree, but a closer look reveals a fundamentally different view, one that is in line with the French tradition of "étatism." Chirac turned out to be not very amused by the idea of a federation:

> Nous ne voulons pas des Etats-Unis d'Europe mais d'une Europe unie des etats (Chirac as quoted in Chayette 2000).

He referred to a statement of former President Charles de Gaulle who had a *Europe des états* (a Europe of states) in mind (De Gaulle 1962: p. 407). In a speech during his visit at the German Bundestag in Berlin, he addressed the mainly Anglo-Saxon nightmare that the process of European integration would not result in a superpower, but in a superstate (Thatcher 1988; Blair 2000):

> Ni vous (the German government, JPvA/FvN) ni nous (the French government, JPvA/FvN) n'envisageons la création d'un super Etat européen qui se substituerait à nos Etats nations et marquerait la fin de leur existence comme acteurs de la vie internationale. Nos nations sont la source de nos identités et de notre enracinement. La diversité de leurs traditions politiques, culturelles et linguistiques est une forces de notre Union. Pour les peuples qui viennent, les nations resteront les premières référence (Chirac 2000).

However, he was sympathetic to the proposal of creating a system of more velocities (more than a "one-speed Europe"), but had a preference for a more informal group of pioneers (Chirac 2000). They both agreed that the principle of subsidiarity (decisions made at the lowest posssible level) would remain in the heart of the European constitution.

In addition, the French prime minister, Lionel Jospin, supported by his minister of finance, Laurent Fabius, used the opportunity of the French presidency to plea for a broader mandate of the Euro–11 by transferring the main responsibility for the anti-inflation policy from the ECB to the Euro–11, which has become the Euro–12 recently, thanks to the entry of Greece, and has been meeting as the "Eurogroup" since the French presidency in the first six months of 2000 (see below).

WHAT ARE THEY DREAMING OF?

One may question what a federation is all about. First, a distinction has to be made between a federation and a confederation, as well as lesser forms of cooperation. A *state* is rooted in representation, defined as a mix of territorial

Territorial / Functional	Variable	Fixed
Variable	Condominio	Consortio
Fixed	Confederatio	Stato/Federatio

Figure 1: A Typology of Modern Polities. Source*: Schmitter 1996.*

and functional constituencies which may be fixed as well as variable (Schmitter 1996). A *federation* is constituted by a constituency that is fixed in both regards.

The classification of Schmitter is not very helpful when it comes to the distinction between a federation and a unitary state, since they are both placed in the same category. A *unitary state* is often associated with a central government in charge of the authoritative allocation, in different functional domains, being congruent with a specific and unique territory (Schmitter 1996: p. 27). The primary characteristic of a *federation* is a division of power between the central and regional government on a territorial basis (Riker 1964: p. 11). In addition, few *secondary* characteristics can be identified, like a written constitution, a bicameral legislature, and a supreme court to protect the constitution (Lijphart 1984; Lijphart 1999).

The American federation as described by Alexis de Tocqueville on his trip through America (1830–1831) is often seen as the pure federation:

> The prerogatives of the federal government were therefore carefully defined and it was declared that everything that was not comprised in that definition returned to the prerogatives of the state governments. Thus the state governments remained the common rule; the federal government was the exception (De Tocqueville 2000: pp. 107–108).

In fact, the division of power has moved away from the original idea of the founding fathers. The two layers of government are not *independent*, but rather *interdependent*, nowadays referred to as *dual* vs. *cooperative* federalism (Landau 1974: p. 174). This constitutes the main distinction between the American and German federation (Scharpf 1988: p. 242), though the American federation has inspired the current German constitution (Siedentop 2000: p. 174), which is marked by what is called "Politikverflechtung" in Germany (Scharpf et al. 1976). The vast majority of the European member states can be qualified as unitary states. Only Austria, Belgium, and Germany can be seen as a federation, though the typology does not count for semi-federal states like Spain or sociologically federal states like The Netherlands.

A federation is often associated with decentralization, but the opposite is true for *the road to* a federation as is shown in the process of European integration.

	Centralized	Decentralized
Federation	Austria	Belgium, Germany
Unitary State	France, Greece, Ireland, Italy, Luxembourg, Portugal, United Kingdom	Denmark, Finland, Sweden

Figure 2: A Categorization of European Member States. Source: *Lijphart 1984*

In most cases federalization means centralization, that is, the transfer of authority and responsibility to a higher level of government. However, centralization is not the only way to create a federation as might be illustrated by the developments in Belgium that have launched a comprehensive program of decentralization, moving away from a semi-federation towards a full federation (1993).

A UNITED STATES OF EUROPE?

Fischer's proposal for a federation was turned down at an informal meeting of the ministers of foreign affairs of the European member states in Evian-les-Bains, France. The minister of foreign affairs of Spain, Josep Piqué i Camps, argued that it made no sense to talk about a *political* union as long as the outcome of the experiment with the *economic* and *monetary* union and the single currency is not clear. A positive experience may have spill-over effects on the willingness to cooperate and integrate in other areas (Bekkers 1995: p. 6). However, we feature all kinds of developments that point toward a federation. The work on the secondary characteristics of a federation is going on, applying once again the method of "fait accompli." The heads of state and prime ministers of the European member states agreed at the Nice summit on a *Charter of Fundamental Rights* that could function as a steppingstone for a written European constitution that includes a clear-cut division of power. The British Prime Minister, Tony Blair. has echoed a plan for the establishment of a European senate introducing bi-cameralism (Blair 2000) and a European court is already in place. The point is that these new institutions may help to create the consensus needed to create a federation, but that such a consensus cannot be reached overnight. It might take decades, most likely, generations. He concludes that a federation is the right goal for Europe, but that Europe is not ready for a federation (Siedentop 2000: p. 231).

Besides, there is nothing new under the sun with regard to the decision to get along with enhanced, flexible cooperation at the Nice summit (2000) as might be illustrated by the Schengen agreement (1985) and, more clearly, the Maastricht treaty (1991) that gave birth to the Economic and Monetary Union. A number of new supranational institutions have been established as part of the Economic and Monetary Union (EMU), notably the European Central Bank (ECB) located in Frankfurt, Germany, pursuing a joint monetary policy in order to avoid inflation in the European member states. In addition, a number of criteria were set for participation in the EMU, like a reduction of the budget deficit, the public debt, the interest rates, and last, but not least, the inflation rates. Furthermore, a procedure was established for the reduction of excessive budget deficits to attain and maintain price stability. In the end, 11 out of 15 countries qualified for the EMU, though only a few states were meeting all the criteria. Notably, Belgium and Italy were running a public debt far above the reference value of 60% of GDP. Only Greece was disqualified. The British and Danish governments called for an opt-out, later followed by Sweden, mainly forced by public opinion giving way to a system of various "speeds" of integration.

The discussion about the first president ,as well as the location of the ECB at the Amsterdam summit (1997), revealed a fundamentally different view on the appropriate role of the new institution (Siedentop 2000). In line with the tradition of "étatism," the French government questioned the independent position of the ECB, which may be seen as a characteristic of a federation: the five central banks with the greatest independence all operate in federal systems (Lijphart 1999: p. 241). France put forward a proposal to create a political watchdog, called Euro–X at that time. It was watered down to an informal meeting at the price of a Resolution on Growth and Employment that provides a framework for the fight against unemployment. The Eurogroup is now (summer 2000) meeting in advance of the meeting of the Council of the European Union in the composition of the ministers of Finance of the European member states. The first item on the agenda of the so-called Economic and Financial Affairs Council (ECOFIN) after the opening of meeting is to fill in the opt-outs about the outcome of the Eurogroup session.

The last addition so far is the decision to create a Eurocorps of about 60,000 troups that may be deployed within 60 days and may be sustained for at least a year to fulfill the so-called Peterburg mission. However, the process of integration will never end in a United States of Europe as Fischer has admitted recently in response to Belgian lawmakers:

> Europe will never be a federation on the US model because it will never have a homogeneous national population. It is made up of different languages, cultures. Building up a US-style system is therefore an illusion (Fischer 2000c).

As a result, mobility of labor will be less than in the American context. Besides, there is still a considerable degree of vitality in the European member states (Berting and Heinemeijer 1995: p. 56).

Finally, subsidiarity will always play a major role in the European situation. It means that a decision should be taken as closely as possible to the citizens (Bekkers et al. 1995: p. 2), that is by the national member states unless the decision power is transferred to one of the supranational institutions. The outcome of the process of European integration, whether it is called a federation, a confederation, or a construction "sui generis" (Lubbers as quoted in Benschop 2000), is as such in line with the striking characterization of Alexis de Tocqueville's original idea of the American federation.

REFERENCES

Bekkers, Victor J.J.M., H.T.P.M. and G. Leenknegt. 1995. (Eds.). *Subsidiariteit en Europese integratie. Een oude wijsheid in een nieuwe context* (Subsidiarity and European Integration. An Old Wisdom in a New Context). W.E.J. Tjeenk Willink: Zwolle.

Benschot, Dick. 2000. *Inleiding over de uitbreiding van de Europese Unie* (Introduction on the enlargement of the European Union, Europa Salon, Clingendael, 's-Gravenhage, 28 juni.

Berting, Jan and Willem F. Heinemeijer. 1995. "'Europe' as a multilevel problem," in: Keebet van Benda-Beckman and Maykel Verkuyten (Eds.), *Nationalism, Ethnicity and Cultural Identity in Europe*, European Research Centre on Migration and Ethnic Relations, Utrecht.

Blair, Tony. 2000. *Europe's Political Future*, speech delivered at the Polish Stock Exchange, Warsaw, October.

Blondel, Jean. 1995 (2nd edition). *Comparative Government. An Introduction*, Prentice Hall/ Harvester Wheatsheaf: London.

Chayette, Silvie. 2000. "Extraits de l'allocution de Jacques Chirac" ("Extracts from a Speech by Jacques Chirac"), *Le Monde* 14 juillet.

Chirac, Jacques. 2000. *Notre Europe*, discours prononce devant le Bundestag, Reichstag: Berlin, June 27.

Conlan, Timothy. 1998. *From New Federalism to Develution. Twenty-Five Years of Intergovernmental Reform*, Brookings Institution Press: Washington.

De Gaulle, Charles. 1962. Conférence de press (press conference) May 15, in: Charles de Gaulle, *Discours et messages*, Plon, Paris 1970, Tome 4 (1962–1965).

De Tocqueville, Alexis. 2000. *Democracy in America*, The University of Chicago Press: Chicago.

Droit, Michel. 1965. Entretien avec Charles de Gaulle (Interview with Charles de Gaulle) 14 décembre, in: Charles de Gaulle, *Discours et messages*, Plon, Paris 1970, Tome 4 (1962–1965).

Elazar, Daniel J. 1995. "From Statism to Federalism: A Paradigm Shift," *Publius* (vol. 25), nr. 2, p. 5–18.

———. (Ed.). 1974. *The Federal Polity*, Center for the Study of Federalism: Philadelphia.

Fischer, Joschka. 2000a. *Vom Staatenverbund zur Föderation—Gedanken über die Finalität der europäischen Integration*, Rede in der Humboldt-Universität in Berlin am 12 Mai.

———. 2000b. *Towards a New Transatlantic Partnership: The United States, Germany and Europe in an Era of Global Challenges*, Herbert Quandt lecture, Georgetown University, September 15.

———. 2000c. "EU Won't Be A Single State Like US", *International Herald Tribune* November 15.

Giscard d'Estaing, and Valéry and Helmut Schmidt. 2000. "La leçon d'Europe" ("The Lesson of Europe"), *Le Figaro*, April 10.

Hénard, Jacqueline, Daniel Vernet, and Roger de Weck. 2000. "La face-à-face Chevènement-Fischer" ("Face to Face: Chevènement vs. Fischer"), *Le Monde/Die Zeit*, June 21, 2000.

Landau, Martin. 1974. "Federalism, Redundancy and System Reliability," in: Elazar, *op. cit.*, pp. 173–196.

Le Boucher, Eric and Laurent Zecchini. 2000. "Jacques Delors critique la stratégie d'élargissement de l'Union" ("Jacques Delors criticizes the enlargement strategy of the [European] Union"), *Le Monde* 19 janvier.

Lijphart, Arend. 1984. *Democracies. Patterns of Majoritarian and Consensus Government in Twenty-One Countries*, Yale University Press: New Haven/London 1984.

———. 1999. *Patterns of Democracy. Government Forms and Performance in Thirty-Six Countries*, Yale University Press: New Haven/London.

Ostrom, Vincent. 1974. "Can Federalism Make a Difference?", in: Elazar, *op. cit.*, pp. 197–238.
——— . 1991. *The Meaning of American Federalism. Constituting a Self-Governing Society*, ICS Press: San Francisco.
Riker, William H. 1964. *Federalism: Origin, Operation, Significance*, Little, Brown and Co: Boston.
Rivlin, Alice. 1992. *Reviving the American Dream. The Economy, the States and the Federal Government*, The Brookings Institution: Washington.
Scharpf, Fritz W. 1978. "Die Theorie der Politikverflechtung. Ein kurzgefaßter Leitfaden" ("The Theory of Joint Decision Making"), in Joachim Jens Hesse (Ed.), *Politikverflechtung im Föderativen Staat (Joint Decision Making in a Federation)*, Nomos: Baden-Baden, pp. 21–31.
——— . 1988. "The Joint-Decision Trap: Lessons From German Federalism and European Integration," *Public Administration* (vol. 66), nr. .., pp. 239–278.
———, Bernd Reissert, and Fritz Schnabel. 1976. *Politikverflechtung: Theorie und Empirie des kooperativen Föderalismus in der Bundesrepublik (Joint Decision Making. Theory and Practice of Cooperative Federalism in Germany)*, Scriptor: Kronberg.
Schmitter, Phillippe C. 1996. "Some alternative futures for the European policy and their implications for European public policy," in: Yves Mény, Pierre Muller and Jean-Louis Quermonne (Eds.), *Adjusting to Europe The Impact of the European Union on National Institutions and Policies*, Routledge: London, pp. 25–40.
Shannon, John and James E. Kee 1989. "The Rise of Competitive Federalism," *Public Budgeting and Finance* (vol. 9), issue 4, pp. 5–20.
Siedentop, Larry. 2000. *Democracy in Europe*, Allen Lane, The Penguin Press: London, etc.
Thatcher, Margaret. 1988. "Britain and Europe," speech delivered at the College of Europe, Bruges, Belgium, September 20.
Van Nispen, Frans K.M. 2000. "The F-word is Back!," preface to *Budgeting for the European Monetarian Union*, Erasmus University of Rotterdam, p. 4.
Verhofstadt, Guy. 2000. "A Vision for Europe," speech to the European Policy Centre, Brussels, September 21.
Watts, Robert L. 1994. "Contemporary views on federalism," in: B. de Villiers (Wd.), *Evaluating Federal Systems*, Martinus Nijhoff: Dordrecht.
Weggeman, Johan. 1997. *Consociatie en federatie. Een literatuurstudie naar hun onderlinge verhouding (A Survey of the Literature on the Interrelation Between Consociation and Federation)*, Rijksuniversiteit: Leiden.
——— . 1998. "Federalisme-onderzoek: nevels en nut," ("Research on Federalism: Smoke and Utility"), *Bestuurskunde* (jrg. 7), nr 8, pp. 368–378.

Chapter 8:

THE CHANGING NATURE OF REGULATION: SOME OBSERVATIONS FROM A SOUTHERN EUROPEAN PERSPECTIVE

Montserrat Cuchillo
University Pompeu Fabra, Barcelona, Spain

INTRODUCTION

"Regulation" does not mean the same thing on both sides of the Atlantic. In fact, "regulation" does not mean the same thing and does not have the same impact in the legal systems of the countries that today constitute the European Union.

Because of these differences, this paper first offers some preliminary observations about the context in which regulatory reform is operating. I then consider the meaning of regulation in the southern European countries on which I concentrate—France, Italy, and Spain—and comment on the implementation of regulation and its impact of European policies in those southern European countries. Finally, I make observations on the adjustment of southern European systems to regulation.

Preliminary Observations about the Context of Regulation

There is considerable regulatory policy change underway in both the US and in the countries belonging to the European Union.

In the US and the EU, the deregulation goals are to guarantee free competition in regulated sectors and to ensure the best possible services for consumers and users. The formulae are also substantially identical: diminution of state and administrative intervention, attribution of the regulation of the sector or industry to independent regulatory bodies, agencies or commissions, and maximization of consumer choice and satisfaction through free competition. But the context in which these formulae are being implemented is, nonetheless, very different, not only on both sides of the Atlantic, but also between countries belonging to the EU.

The basic difference between the US and the EU is in the departure point. In the US, contemporary regulatory policies and commissions have a secular tradition and are centered in free competition as a guarantee of the satisfaction of consumer interests.

In EU countries, on the other hand, the departure point is the existence of private economic activities, some of which are subject to "police" powers while others are subject to "service public" rules, and economic activities developed by public corporations subject to "service public" rules. Rule-making and control of such activities fully belong to administrative organisms integrated in the state apparatus. Regulatory policies implemented in the '80s and '90s dramatically altered the situation. They required, first, the privatization of activities formerly subject to "service public" rules and, second, the application of regulation to certain private activities that had been subject to less stringent "police" powers. Finally, they required the reform of public administration modeled on US regulatory commissions and independents agencies.

Beyond these differences between the US and the EU countries, there are also differences among the countries belonging to the EU.

Great Britain,adheres to the logic of common law, while in continental Europe the administrative law tradition (often known as civil law in the US) is dominant. It should also be pointed out that since the end of World War II and beginning with the German constitution, European countries, with the exception of Great Britain, have remodeled their political systems with the establishment of constitutional courts and constitutional controls (Meny 1993).

In the southern European countries on wish I want to focus—Spain, Italy, and France—constitutional reform (and the new balance of power that its working generates) took place during the 1970s and the beginning of the 1980s. Constitutional reform runs parallel to a deep reform of state structures, translated into devolution of relevant powers and functions to regional and local authorities (Sharpe 1993). I shall return later to the influence of the administrative law tradition and its impact on developments in the institutional setting in the implementation of regulatory reform, from the mid-1980s onward in France, Italy, and Spain. But first, let's review the meaning of regulation in these southern European countries to help clarify my later comments.

The Absence of A Notion of Regulation in Southern European Countries Until the Mid-'80s

One may recall that, in the US, regulation could be defined as sustained and focused control exercised by public agencies over activities developed by individuals, groups, or firms considered as desirable to society. Regulation and control of these activities is not left to legislators and bureaucrats but assigned to specialized organisms, regulatory commissions or independent agencies, with deep knowledge of the activities, capable of fact-finding, rule-making, and enforcement (Pierce and Gellhorn 1982).

From a legal perspective, the notion of regulation remits to control of private firms. Some activities fall under "public utilities regulation" while others do not. But regulation implies control in relation to price, output, and/or product quality in an effort to prevent purely private decisionmaking that would not take adequate consideration of "public interest." Conflicts and controversies regarding regulated activities are subject to judicial review by state or federal courts according to the general rules that determine jurisdiction (Breyer and Stewart 1985).

Regulatory policies are promulgated on the necessity to perfect legislative "correction" of market failures. They were originally designed (Interstate Commerce Commission 1887) to advance accepted goals of reliability and, in particular, non-discrimination. From the '80s onward, regulation has been oriented toward the promotion of competition and the maximization of consumer choice (Kearny and Merrill 1998).

In any case, the focus on market logic and market failure generally excludes agencies whose primary mission is distributive or redistributive from theories of regulation (Croley 1998).

Until the mid-1980s, in southern European countries the notion of regulation was "purely and simply ignored by the law" (Timsit 1996). What in the US fell into the field of regulation, fell into general "governmental action" embodied in two basic categories: "police" and "public service." Neither of these categories fully corresponds to regulation and both operate upon private activities that would be subject to regulation in the US.

Thus, licensing and authorizations in the field of drugs and pharmaceutical products were subject to "police" powers. Regulated industries and services in the US such as telecommunications and railways were subject to the rules of public service that also applied to services excluded by regulatory policies in the US, such as public health and public education. A variety of economic activities developed by public corporations in fields as diverse as tourism, funerary services, and the general promotion of economic and social and welfare of the community (Sorace 1998, Cuchillo 1998, Terneyre 1998) faired similarly.

The reasons whereby a given private activity effected a public interest or became considered as desirable to society is subject to police powers or to public service rules as diverse as the activities to which they apply. Many are caused by history and tradition, or by social and political and ideological evolution, though sometimes happenstance is a more plausible explanation (Marcou 1995). But a line defining subjection to public service rules could be drawn that would include, on the one hand, strategic activities and industries, such as petrol, steel, mining, transportation, telecommunications and postal services. On the other hand, it would include, on the basis of the need to protect the public interest, the development, by public corporations of activities belonging to the field reserved by nineteenth-century liberalism for private entrepreneurs (Sorace 1999). The basic difference between activities subject to police powers and to public service consists in their conception as private activities, as opposed to public activities.

The immediate legal consequences of the distinction can be summarized as follows. The first group of activities is regulated by private law, and the resolution of conflicts and controversies regarding those activities is lodged with ordinary courts. The public service activities, whether developed by public corporations or by private enterprises exercising a monopoly or under restricted competence rules fixed by the concession of public service techniques, are submitted to administrative law and conflicts and controversies are lodged with administrative law courts. In France, the submission to the administrative law regime does not entail the intervention of specialized courts (*contencioso-administrativo*) as is the case in Italy and Spain, but of the so-called *juges administratifs*, that is, of public officials belonging to the state apparatus, whose decisions are reconsidered, in case of an appeal, by a governmental organism: the *Conseil d'Etat*.

The Administrative State Crisis, European Integration and the Meaning of Regulation after the Mid-1980s in Southern European Countries

The legitimacy crisis of the administrative state developed on both sides of the Atlantic at essentially the same time. But in France, Italy, and Spain, redistributive politics through taxation and discretionary macroeconomic management were dominant until the mid-1980s.

Regulatory reform, underway in the US and GB since the late '70s, emerged as the solution to the failures of the system, including those responsible for the fiscal crisis of the state and its most poignant consequences: unemployment and inflation (Majone 1997).

By the mid-1980s, the critical character of the situation, converging with globalization and projects for economic and monetary integration within the European Union, made conditions favorable for a generalized reception of regulatory reform. The so-called positive state and its corollaries, unlimited power to tax and to spend, was to be fundamentally changed through privatization, regulatory policies, and an increase of market-based mechanisms to fulfill administrative obligations.

In southern European countries, and deriving from these developments, a generalized reception of terms such as "regulation," "regulatory state," and "regulatory reform" took place—not only by economists and political scientists familiar with Anglo-Saxon terminology, but also by politicians, public officials, and legal scholars belonging to the "administrative law" tradition where, as I have already mentioned, "regulation" has no legal meaning at all.

In this context, and from a legal perspective, regulation is understood with no differentiation between "public utilities regulation" and "regulation" *tout court*, as a form of state intervention that departs from classic coercive and imperative institutions and procedures. In relation to other authoritarian legal rules and provisions, regulation would entail incentive rather than coercive measures, more flexible procedures and a higher degree of participation in decisionmaking and conflict resolution (Miaille 1991, Timsit 1996).

Regulation implies the use of measures and the establishment of rules that are internalized and accepted by the subjects of regulation itself, as they become co-authors of the norms and legal provisions according to which activities are regulated, norms enforced, and conflicts resolved. Guidance, directives, participation of the subjects involved in public bodies or mixed administrations responsible for organization and control, and the transfer of some functions to citizens and consumers are some of the instruments whereby internalization takes place (Majone 1992, OECD 1996).

But apart from these very vague and general ideas, no real effort has been made to translate the new terminology into the logic of the administrative law system in which the concepts it transmits is going to operate. A few works, however, do deserve to be mentioned, among which are those of professors Timsit (1994, 1996) and Miaille (1992, 1996) in France, and Sorace (1999) in Italy.

With this, I do not mean to say that the impact of regulatory reform in European countries has not been the object of substantial attention or of many excellent studies. I simply mean to emphasize that regulatory institutions have been incorporated without the necessary attention given to the difficulties derived from the application of their logic to activities that for nearly a century had been subject to the logic of public service within administrative law systems. Indeed, without this close attention, to some degree, the advantages of regulatory techniques are lost. "We are dealing with a veritable non-concept, to which the law gives no place forbidding, in such way, the recognition of a scientific status that would allow the generalized use of the measures regulation entails in the process of streamlining and reform of the administrative apparatus" (Timsit, 1996).

Institutional and Regulatory Reform in Southern European Countries and the Impact of European Integration

Institutional Reform in the 1970s and 1980s: Constitutional Reform and Devolution of powers

As mentioned earlier, during the 1970s and the beginning of the 1980s important institutional reforms took place in Spain, Italy, and France. These reforms entailed constitutional changes that run parallel to devolution of relevant powers and functions to regional and local authorities.

Constitutional reform brought with it the establishment of constitutional courts, with different functions in France, Italy, and Spain. But a common consequence emerged: increased attention to individual rights and liberties and also a relevant increase in the recognition and protection of collective and/or diffuse rights and interests. These collective rights were very often connected or assimilated to the right to have access to certain goods and services that were provided, in most cases, according to public service rules (Meny 1993).

In this context, and with access to power of socialist governments in Spain, Italy, and France, a number of collective goods and services that until then had not been provided by governmental institutions, were granted to most citizens during the '70s and '80s. In fact, Italy, and Spain went to the point of constitutionally entrenching the right of citizens to have access to some of those services. In France, public service literature stressed the transformation of the role of the state, from the exercise of power (*puissance publique*) to the provision of services (Chevallier 1987). The state derived an important degree of legitimacy through the provision and/or organization and control of such services, as it was viewed by large sectors of the population as the only guaranteed alternative to the egoistic interests of money in the setting of 40–60% societies.

Devolution processes developed in France, Italy, and Spain along constitutional reform processes. They entailed the establishment of intermediate levels of government with legislative and executive powers in Italy and in Spain, and the devolution of executive powers and functions to local authorities in France. Most of the functions assigned to regional and local governmental levels were not so much the provision of strategic facilities, but of the goods and services nearest to the community.

Devolution meant the empowerment of regional and local authorities to define local policies and to provide local services with a large degree of autonomy in relation to central government. In Spain and Italy one of the mechanisms whereby these governmental institutions assumed a relevant role in public life in a relatively short time was the creation of a vast and complex administrative structure and of a large bureaucracy, as well as an expansion of the provisions of public goods and services (Cuchillo 1993, Cassese and Torchia 1993).

Decentralization and devolution literature has stressed democratic values forwarded by devolution. Since their establishment, regional and local tiers of government in southern European countries have succeeded in attaining a relevant degree of legitimacy from their capacity to make policies in accordance with community interests and from their ability to adjust them to changing needs and preferences (Meny 1985, Sharpe 1993).

Regulatory Reform from the Mid-1980s until the Mid-1990s

Regulatory reform literature was translated into regulatory reform policies that entailed deep state reform in France, Italy, and Spain between the mid-1980s and the mid-1990s.

The incorporation of the ideas of the so-called regulatory state meant the breaking up of public or private monopolies in sectors such as the supply of petrol or postal services, railway, and telephone services; the privatization of public companies responsible for services such as water, gas, and electricity supply; and the establishment of competitive tendering in many regulated sectors until then subject to the logic of public service. These measures were accompanied by the establishment of mixed organizations, modeled on regulatory commissions and independent agencies. Conflicts were lodged with those organisms remitting final decisions to judicial review.

In France, Italy, and Spain, regulatory reform substantially altered the traditional organization of public administration and restricted the functions assigned to governmental bodies. But it did not alter the administrative law system and its logic. That is to say, the concept of public administration as the state apparatus responsible for the satisfaction of public or general interests, as opposed to private and egoistic interests, and the concept of administrative law as the legal order best adapted to the fulfillment of such functions (Caillosse 1996) remained unchanged.

Thus, regulatory organisms were established with a deeper connection to public administration than is usual in the US. The degree of independence of its members from the government of the day is lessened regarding designation, permanence in their condition, and decisionmaking capability. These organisms have to develop many of their most relevant functions, namely regulation and control, according to administrative law rules, and when competitive tendering is imposed, it is administrative law that rules. Accordingly, conflicts regarding regulation, control of regulated activities, and competitive tendering are to be resolved on appeal by administrative courts (or by the *juge administratif*, in France) applying administrative law rules and principles.

In a way, it could be maintained that regulatory techniques were applied to activities subject to public service rules. But many of these rules, together with constitutional and principles providing state intervention, proved to be more resilient to change than anticipated. And the traditional mentality of public officials, legal scholars, and magistrates specializing in administrative law, proved to be more resilient to the new regulatory institutions they had to deal with than the old public service for which they were meant to substitute.

Regulatory Reform and European Integration

The establishment of the European Union and, especially, the sanction of the Treaty of Amsterdam in 1997, marked an inflection point in the pace of regulatory reform in France, Italy, and Spain. The Treaty imposed the submission to free competition rules "of all corporations, public or private, responsible for services of general economic interest, as long as the logic of competition is not an obstacle to the development of the specific mission they serve" (articles 16 and 86 of the Treaty). Conflicts regarding accordance with European principles being thus transferred from state courts to the European court of justice European integration necessarily requires a readjustment of member state institutions and policies (Mény 1996).

The enforcement of provisions on services of general economic interests requires a very relevant adjustment that is not proving to be an easy operation in southern European countries—especially due to the fact that the dismantling of the public service structure has been resented by a number of factions. Institutional reforms that took place during the '70s and '80s contributed to the building of resistance to the enforcement of European directives on the one hand because the legitimacy crisis of the state that generated tough criticism based on inefficiency, waste of resources, and bureaucratization was somewhat minimized by the consideration of the state as the basic guarantee of general interests face to egoistic economic power.

The founding of European directives lies initially on the establishment of a common market through free competition and free circulation of persons, goods, and capital. Directives stress the fact that regulation and growing reliance on market-based managerial practices ensures better service delivery and higher consumer satisfaction, and have established provisions regarding universal access to essential services in most sectors that, in the US, would fall into "public utilities" regulation. But these practices are not easily accepted as legitimate in a context secularly steered by the reliance on public bodies for the satisfaction of general interests, especially, when following constitutional reform, substantial collective rights, and interests have been ensured through public service.

Devolution further complicated the application of European directives and the implementation of subsequent regulatory reform. Regulatory reform according to European directives necessarily means a restriction of the functions assigned to regional and local government and to their administrative organizations, and a diminution of their visibility and legitimacy in relation to their communities. Regional and local governments and their administrative organizations have thus tended to be reluctant to full implementation of European regulatory provisions

Some Observations About the Impact of Regulation in Southern European Countries

The logic of regulation and of regulatory reform has been adopted in southern European countries with alacrity and according to criteria that preserve the substantial differences between the regime of regulated industries and activities in France, Italy, and Spain and in other European countries and, indeed, in relation to the US.

Regulatory reform has substantially altered the structure and functions of public administration in France, Italy, and Spain. But the logic of regulation has such a deep impact on the founding principles of state action that regulatory institutions have been "corrected" or "adapted" to those principles. This is due to the fact that subjection to free competition rules and adoption of market-based practices threaten to alter the founding principles of the state and of the legal order. This is because the state and its administrative structure are no longer immediately responsible for the provision and protection of "public and general" interests and because the administrative law system is no longer justified, as the departure from the principles and rules applying to private subjects had been founded on the need to allow the fulfillment of governmental functions regarding the "public and general" interests.

The ability of administrative law to renounce the privileges and exceptions to private law rules and principles implies an imperfect application of regulatory mechanisms. Some legal regulatory measures have not been fully enforced. Among them the following may be mentioned: procedures for the defense of individual and collective rights and interests through provisions regarding legal actions, remedies and standing rules, and affordable legal assistance to litigants; adequate control of private companies and protection of free competition through publicity and astringent anti-trust provisions; and transparency and hard-look review of regulatory rule-making and control.

The imperfect translation of the logic of regulation, due to the imperfect adaptation of institutional and legal mechanisms, makes it more difficult, and sometimes impossible, for regulatory policies to accomplish the goals that they are supposed to serve. In turn, the poor performance of regulatory techniques makes it more difficult for regulation to be accepted.

In fact, it could be said that in southern European countries regulation means more than reorganization of the state and of the administrative organization. Regulation means a new conception of political and social institutions. Regulatory reform requires a change of mentality—not only on the part of politician and public officials, but also on the part of entrepreneurs and private firms, used to a privileged relationship with public bodies, and on the part of large sectors of the population that view neo-liberal values as exclusively centered on profit and economic incentives and, in many ways, as incompatible with community interests and values.

REFERENCES

Breyer, S. and Stewart, R. 1982. *Administrative Law and Regulatory Policies.* Boston: Little, Brown & Co. Second edition.

Caillosse, J. 1986. "Dret Public et Droit Privé: Sens et Portee d'un Partage Academique." *ADJA*, December.

Cassese, S. and L.Torchia. 1993. "Regions as the Italian Meso." In L.J. Sharpe (Ed.), *The Rise of Meso Government : Developments at the Meso Level in Europe*. London: Sage.

Chevallier, J. 1987. *Le Service Public.* Paris: PUF.

Cuchillo, M. 1993. "The Autonomous Communities as the Spanish Meso." In L.J. Sharpe (Ed.), *The Rise of Meso Government: Developments at the Meso Level in Europe*. London: Sage.

———. 2000. "Le Droit Espagnol." In Troper, M. (Ed.). *Interventionisme Economique et Pouvoir Local en Europe*. Paris: Economica.

Kearney, J.D. and T.W. Merrill. 1998. "The Great Transformation of Regulated Industries Law," *Col. L. Rev.* 98.

Majone, G. 1997. *From the Positive to the Regulatory State: Causes and Consequences of Changes in the Mode of Governance.* Madrid: Estudios. CEACS.

———. 1992. *Deregulation or Re-regulation? Regulatory Reform in Europe and the United States.* London: Pinter.

Marcou, G. (Ed.). 1995. *Les Mutations du Droit de l'Administration en Europe*. Paris: L'harmattan.

Mazey, S. 1993. "Regional and local authorities as the French Meso." In L.J. Sharpe (Ed.), *The Rise of Meso Government: Developments at the Meso Level in Europe*. London: Sage.

Meny, Y. 1993. *Politique Compare des Democraties: Allemagne, Etats-Unis, France, Grande-Bretagne, Italie.* Paris: Montchrestien, Fourth edition.

———. 1996. *Adjusting to Europe: The impact of the EU in National Institutions and Policies.* London: Routledge

Miaille, M. 1991. *La Regulation et le Pouvoir Politique.* Barcelona: ICPS.

———. 1993. *La Regulation, entre Politique et Droit* Paris: L'harmattan.

OECD Working Papers. 1996. *Regulatory Reform: Overview and Proposed OECD Working Plan*. Paris.

Pierce, E. and R. Gellhorn. 1982. *Regulated Industries Law.* St. Paul: West Publishing. Third edition.

Sharpe, L.J. (Ed.). 1993. *The Rise of Meso Government: Developments at the Meso Level in Europe*. London: Sage.

Sorace, D. 2000. "Le Droit Italien." In M. Troper (Ed,). *Interventionisme Economique et Pouvoir Local en Europe*. Paris: Economica.

———. "Servici Pubblici e Servizi (Economici) di Pubblica Utilità in Diritto Pubblico," no. 2.

Terneyre, F. "Le Droit Italien." In M. Troper (Ed.). *Interventionisme Economique et Pouvoir Local en Europe*. Paris: Economica.

Timsit, G. 1996. "Les Deux Corps du Droit. Essai sur la Notion de Regulation." *Revue Francaise d'Administration Publique*, no. 78.

Chapter 9:

GLOBAL TRADE SOVEREIGNTY AND SUBNATIONAL AUTONOMY

David Eaton
Lyndon B. Johnson School of Public Affairs, The University of Texas at Austin

INTRODUCTION

Over the past 50 years, and particularly during the past decade, nations have sought to expand international commerce by removing trade barriers, both the physical and procedural variety at border crossings, as well as substantive laws and regulations that restrict equal access of firms in one nation to the markets of another. Any international trade agreement restricts national sovereignty and local autonomy, particularly laws and regulations related to food, agriculture, environment, resource management, health, and economic development. International trade agreements typically seek to remove discrimination between local origin products and services and those from others. Some trade agreements protect local rules through selective exceptions or reservations. It remains to be seen whether the emerging international law undergirding trade will improve or undermine democracy at the state and local levels.

TRADE AND SUBNATIONAL AUTONOMY

Since World War II, nations sought to encourage multilateral commerce by reducing or removing trade barriers. The various negotiation rounds under the

General Agreement on Tariffs and Trade (GATT), particularly GATT–1994, the European Union, the North American Free Trade Agreement (NAFTA), World Trade Organization (WTO) discussions, and other multilateral forums have sought to free capital and labor by facilitating equal access to markets. Some analysts believe that this past decade's sustained economic expansion reflects the increased opportunities made possible by the international trade system. Despite challenges to this process by the Seattle and Washington, D.C. demonstrations this past year, the process of trade liberalization continues. Even once-protective nations (such as Argentina, China, and even Switzerland) today are keen to join the system. The pace is increasing within the European Union (EU), as it adopts the Euro and considers admitting 12 or 13 new members through the "accession" process.

One necessary consequence of multilateral trade agreements is that actions which level the playing field by allowing equal access to markets simultaneously restrict traditional national sovereignty and local autonomy. There are two key provisions common in most comprehensive multilateral trade agreements, such as those associated with the EU, GATT, WTO, and NAFTA: a nondiscrimination clause and national implementation obligations.

Many comprehensive multilateral trade agreements prohibit preferences for local suppliers that discriminate against trading partners. There are several common discrimination issues (see Table 1): origin, production method, quantitative limits, elective rules, risk regulations, and direct subsidies. To assure

Table 1: Common Trade Agreement Restrictions on Discrimination

Rule	*Application*
No discrimination by national origin	Equal access of foreign suppliers to a local market
No discrimination by production process	Limits on labor origin or content requirements
No trade restrictive rules	Limits on packaging, labeling, or safety rules
No risks standards not science-based	Food safety, commercial quality, food processing, or label requirements
No direct subsidies affecting competition	Tax classification, tax deductions, or procurement incentives

Source: Modified from Stumberg, Robert. "Balancing Democracy and Trade: The Report of GATT in NAFTA on State Law," in Eaton, D. (Ed.), 1996, *The Impacts of Trade Agreements on State and Provincial Laws*, Lyndon B. Johnson School of Public Affairs, Austin: The University of Texas at Austin, TX, pp. 52–56.

equal access by foreign suppliers to local markets, trade agreements limit preferences as to the origin of goods. Local content rules, such as labor origin standards, are controlled. Rules on packaging, labeling, or safety that could restrict equal access by non-local suppliers are prohibited. Limits on commercial fishing, animal import, vehicle loads, or other quantitative rules that restrict market access are limited. Environmental or safety standards can be restricted, even those tied to food safety, food processing, or labeling. Subsidies that unfairly promote local suppliers may be restricted; examples would be tax classification, tax deductions, procurement content rules, or natural resource-use incentives.

Not only do multilateral trade agreements restrict local autonomy, but also they usually require each national government pit its trade obligations against local priorities. The Vienna Convention on the Law of Treaties (Articles 27 and 29) codifies the principle of sovereignty over the whole of a national territory: a treaty is binding upon the entire territory of each signatory and no signatory may invoke an internal law to justify treaty noncompliance unless a different intention is included explicitly in the treaty. Some trade agreements go beyond this passive formulation to impose positive obligations upon national signatories to compel subnational implementation. For example, Articles XXII, XXIII, and XXIV of GATT–1994 require each signatory to take "reasonable measures" to assure that subnational authorities within its territory abide by all provisions. The NAFTA goes further, requiring signatories to take "all necessary measures" to assure that provincial, state, and local governments implement NAFTA. EU accession rules are even stronger: no country may accede to the EU unless all national and subnational legislation and standards have previous to accession been harmonized with applicable EU directives, rules, and regulations.

Nondiscrimination, combined with the national obligation to enforce trade treaty obligations on subnational governments, may affect the autonomy of states, provinces, and local governments, and even impinge upon national sovereignty. Table 2 lists some of the rules and regulations that may be affected by multilateral trade agreements. Some of the arenas of local or provincial regulation likely to be affected include food quality, food packaging, food inspection, toxic contents limits, pollution standards, wildlife protection, energy or water conservation, procurement rules, export promotion, and business assistance.

The tension between multilateral trade and local autonomy in these areas are visible already in the arguments over British or American beef, genetically enhanced seeds, French sparkling water, or Spanish and Italian wines. Just the potential risk that multinational corporations could develop a free hand to flaunt local health, safety, environmental, or labor standards was one of the factors in free-trade related demonstrations in Seattle and Washington, D.C. during the past eight months.

Even as trade agreements tend to prohibit new local or state regulations that could restrict equal access to markets, some agreements contain provisions to

Table 2: Regional and Local Rules or Regulations Affected By Multilateral Trade Agreements

Topic	*Examples*
Food quality	Fruit or vegetable standards Animal feed content Seed contents and labels Milk and frozen dessert classifications
Food packaging	Ingredient labels Origin of citrus products Organic farm standards Kosher content labeling Use or ban of materials (e.g., plastics)
Food inspection	Meat inspection rules Shellfish inspection rules Workplace sanitation rules
Toxic contents limits	Pesticide limits or inspection Toxic contents limits Pesticide use Tableware, wine bottles, and packaging toxic limits Construction materials limits (asbestos or lead)
Pollution standards	Air, water, and noise discharge limits Solvent, fuel, or aerosol standards Recycling content requirements
Wildlife protection	Endangered species import limits Wild animal import limits Fishing practices
Energy or water conservation	Alternative fuel subsidies Oil, gas, or coal conservation Green energy subsidies Water conservation rules
Procurement rules	National, in-state, or local purchasing preferences Minority preferences Local representation
Export promotion	Marketing or financing of local exports Customized or subsidized job training Tax incentives
Business assistance	Small business subsidies Infrastructure subsidies Tax incentives (job creation, investment)

Source: Modified from Stumberg, Robert. "Balancing Democracy and Trade: The Report of GATT in NAFTA on State Law," in D. Eaton (Ed.), 1996, *The Impacts of Trade Agreements on State and Provincial Laws*, Lyndon B. Johnson School of Public Affairs, Austin: The University of Texas at Austin, TX, pp. 52–56.

protect long-established local rules. For example, Articles 1108 and 1206 of NAFTA allow states or provinces to list non-conforming statutes (existing rules in contravention to NAFTA) that could be "reserved" or allowed to remain after NAFTA. The two NAFTA side agreements on labor and the environment do not require changes in existing standards, but do obligate each signatory to enforce its own laws. NAFTA allows local autonomy on environmental, health, and safety standards that are so-called "science-based." However, trade panels and the courts have yet to define in operational terms how much science is sufficient and at what stage should it be introduced within the standards-setting process.

In addition to the regulatory protections in trade agreements, there are two types of procedural safeguards to local autonomy. These processes are political action and the glacial process of trade dispute resolution.

Subnational jurisdictions can draw national attention to potential problems and, through that leverage, resolve them. For example, NAFTA obliges signatories to take all "necessary" measures to implement the agreement by state and local jurisdictions. GATT trade panels had interpreted "necessary" as "least trade restrictive," wording which per se would undermine state environmental standards. US states used their political skills to influence the wording of NAFTA's "Statement of Administrative Action" to articulate that "necessary" does not mean " least trade restrictive," so that trade panels cannot be bound by the least protective environmental standards.

A second process protection is that any challenge to subnational rules follows a slow, four-stage process: mandatory informal negotiations, filing of the trade dispute, referral to a trade panel, and formal argument before the trade panel. Even in the event of a finding against a subnational unit, the national government would be placed in the uncomfortable posture of having to sue its subnational unit to enforce; such a suit is rare under any legal system. It is more likely that the nation damaged would gain a right to take countervailing action—otherwise known as trade sanctions—against the offending subnational unit. This process allows the state or province to weigh the costs of trade sanctions versus the benefits to the offending standard.

EXPERIENCE WITH TRADE AGREEMENT IMPLEMENTATION

It is beyond the scope of this paper to discuss the degree to which trade panels or the courts have found that multilateral treaties trump national, state, or local rules. It would be worthwhile to discuss some of the diverse results, to at least indicate how uncertain are the outcomes of trade equity challenges to national or subnational legislation or negotiation.

In the American context there have been at least three panel decisions and one recent court decision that set limits to local autonomy under a multilateral trade agreement. In 1991, a GATT dispute resolution panel ruled that the US Marine Mammal Protection Act (a law that bans the sale of tuna caught by fishing methods that kill too many dolphins) was inconsistent with the GATT. That Act remains US law and Congress has even strengthened it. In 1992, in the so-called Beer II case, a GATT panel found that Canada had not taken "all reasonable" measures to assure that Ontario did not give tax breaks to local breweries or exempt them from common carrier requirements. The US response, as the aggrieved party, was to impose countervailing duties on Ontario's exports, a process which motivated Ontario to alter its measures. In 1994, the US both levied a tax on large cars, the so-called "gas guzzler tax," and created corporate average fuel economy standards. Those rules, challenged as discriminatory based on country of origin, were justified as necessary to protect life, health, as well as conserve exhaustible natural resources. In a recent case, earlier in 2000 a federal court disallowed a state prohibition on trade with Burma; the matter is still under litigation.

This experience with trade panels and the courts does not provide clear guidelines as to what will occur when international trading partners challenge state or local regulations or rules in the US. These results are also no guide to the consequences of trade-related challenges in other nations.

CONCLUSIONS

Multilateral trade agreements are likely to change subnational government roles. Global trade is creating an imperative for the rule of multinational law as a means to secure mobility of trade, capital, labor, and services. It is hard to know whether such change will be beneficial or harmful to the citizens who are subject to the affected state, regional, or local jurisdiction. Trade agreements do not set common international standards, but rather seek to secure a so-called "equal" playing field: local products are not allowed to have structural advantages over foreign products. However, it is clear that trade can facilitate common international standards for either good or ill, compromise the sovereignty of national governments, and reduce the autonomy of provincial, state, and regional, or local governments.

ACKNOWLEDGEMENTS

This paper has drawn from contributors to Eaton, David J. (Ed.), 1996, *The Impacts of Trade Agreements on State and Provincial Laws,* Austin, TX: The University of Texas at Austin. Those contributors include Ira Shapiro (pp. 7–9), Peter Fawcett (pp. 10–12), David Morel (pp. 16–20), Amanda Atkinson (pp. 47–51), Helmut Mach (pp. 57–60) and, particularly, Robert Stumberg (pp. 52–56). Preparation of this paper was supported by grants from the US Department of the Army, the US Information Agency, the US Department of Education, the Canadian Embassy of Canada to the United States, and the Lyndon Baines Johnson School of Public Affairs of The University of Texas at Austin.

MIX
Papier aus verantwortungsvollen Quellen
Paper from responsible sources
FSC® C105338

If you have any concerns about our products,
you can contact us on
ProductSafety@springernature.com

In case Publisher is established outside the EU,
the EU authorized representative is:
Springer Nature Customer Service Center GmbH
Europaplatz 3, 69115 Heidelberg, Germany

Printed by Libri Plureos GmbH
in Hamburg, Germany